Chances Are . . .

PROVIDENCE? SERENDIPITY? OR FATE?

Chances Are . . .

PROVIDENCE? SERENDIPITY? OR FATE?

Edited by Carol S. Lawson & Robert F. Lawson

CHRYSALIS BOOKS / *Swedenborg Foundation Publishers*
West Chester, Pennsylvania

THE CHRYSALIS READER is a book series that examines themes related to the universal quest for wisdom. Inspired by the writings of Swedenborg, each volume presents original short stories, essays, poetry, and art exploring the spiritual dimensions of a chosen theme. Works are selected by the series editors. For information on future themes or submission of original writings, contact Carol S. Lawson, Route 1, Box 4510, Dillwyn, Virginia 23936.

Printed on recycled paper and bound in the United States of America.

LIBRARY OF CONGRESS CATALOGING-IN-PUBLICATION DATA
Chances are . . . providence? serendipity? or fate? / edited by Carol S. Lawson
& Robert F. Lawson.
p. cm. — (Chrysalis reader ; v. 9)
ISBN 0-87785-233-2
1. Chance—Literary collections. 2. Providence and government of God—Literary collections. 3. Fate and fatalism—Literary collections. 4. Serendipity—Literary collections. 5. American literature—21st century.
I. Title: Chances are. II. Lawson, Carol S. III. Lawson, Robert F., 1948–
IV. Series
PS509.C47 C47 2002
810.8'0384—dc21

2002071406

CHRYSALIS BOOKS
Swedenborg Foundation Publishers
320 North Church Street
West Chester, Pennsylvania 19380

Contents

EDITOR'S NOTE: ROBERT F. LAWSON

Serendipity in Action

The Feast of Sadeh: Leaf from a Shah-nameh. Colors, ink, silver, and gilt on paper, 1520–1522 period, Reign of Shah Tahmasp. The Metropolitan Museum of Art. Gift of Arthur A. Houghton Jr., 1970.

BLANCHE MOYSE, co-founder of the Marlboro Music Festival and renowned conductor of Bach, tells her singers, "You are the notes. The notes are there because you are feeling something."[1] Moyse's advice is an apt analogy of the influx of spiritual reality in one's life. Just as her singers must be open to the influence of Bach's music in order to register the emotion above the printed page, so too must spiritual seekers be receptive to the inner life of spirit in order to resonate with the spiritual life that permeates the natural world. As

Wilson Van Dusen explains, our relationship to the order of existence depends on our harmonizing what is in us with what is outside us.

Spiritual growth, according to Swedenborg, is a two-way street. Yes, we grow toward the light, but it's tricky business, our meeting the spirit. There is a potent immediacy of the spiritual moment in which we choose to act. It takes celestial timing and then something more. We must respond from the heart, from our ruling love. So despite everything, despite our best-laid plans, our well-thought-out intentions, some of our greatest gains occur when we least expect it. Seemingly unconnected events fall together of their own accord to positively impact our lives. Great strides may come in those serendipitous moments when our spiritual receptors are caught unaware by the nurturing influence of divine forces.

Chances Are . . . Providence? Serendipity? or Fate? explores this paradox of spiritual growth when life-defining events happen in the serendipitous currents outside our mainstream experience. Can it be coincidence? Or is there a master plan of divine design? What forces mold and direct us without our conscious participation? How do we respond and how do we know when we are being led by the spirit or by our own invention?

We share, for example, the experience of an author who chances upon a woman, still alive, though entombed in a snow-bound car. Was there a reason, a divine leading, that influenced the author to take that particular road at that particular hour?

Through this collection of essays, short stories, poetry, and art, *Chances Are . . .* examines the possibilities of chance and divine providence in the swirling dance of ordinary and extraordinary circumstances, events in which we *must* respond in order to live fully. Readers will follow on the heels of life-and-death decisions made by workers as World Trade Tower 2 implodes, experience the uncertainty of WW II combat soldiers, and make a desperate run for freedom with an American citizen as he is swept up by political turmoil in 1914 Mexico City.

We also encounter a spiritual awakening, tingling like a tuning fork, at France's holy shrine in Lourdes. The shadow side of serendipity is acknowledged on a foggy night close to home in New England, and then at a Nagasaki memorial. We re-live issues of hope and trust, of being open and alert, at a balloon ascension in Ohio, and again in a hotel room filled with a network of family and relatives come to hear how one of their kin died half a century ago on a distant battlefield.

What role does chance or fate play in spiritual growth? If we are born with dual citizenship—both earthly and spiritual—perhaps it is through an energizing mix of free will, circumstance, and divine providence that we grow into full citizenship of both communities. *Chances Are . . .* sheds light on forces that mold and direct us throughout the surprising dance of spiritual growth.

Note

1. Benjamin Ivry, "Her Gestures Draw Emotion—and Crowds," *The Christian Science Monitor,* 21 June 2002, 19.

A comment on the word origin of serendipity: Our current use of serendipity—the making of providential or happy discoveries, the acquisition of valuable things not sought for—has grown from its first application by Horace Walpole, British writer and historian, who coined the word in 1754. Walpole took the word from the title of a book *The Three Princes of Serendip* (formerly Ceylon, now Sri Lanka)—a sixteenth-century collection of Indian and Persian folklore known as the *Peregrinaggio*—which he read as a child. Walpole recalled how the three astute and perceptive brothers had the ability to make keen deductions from chance discoveries while in search of something else, and used his new word in that sense.

The brothers' uncanny ability comes to the fore early in the *Peregrinaggio* when, after arriving at their first destination, the brothers make Sherlockian pronouncements about a missing camel. Never having seen the camel, they nevertheless have noted its progress on the highway and ask its owner, a camel driver, if it is blind in one eye, missing a tooth, and is lame. The owner hurries off to find the camel but shortly returns empty-handed. The brothers then complete the description, saying that the stray camel is carrying a load of butter on one side, and honey on the other. To the consternation of its owner, they add that its human mount is a pregnant woman. So accurate are their pronouncements, the camel driver is convinced the brothers have stolen his animal and implores the local ruler to imprison them as highwaymen and thieves.

Of course, since this is the first of many adventures, the brothers are soon released from prison when the missing camel is located. The brothers then reveal the evidence from which they have made their deductions, and the chagrined ruler realizes he is in the presence of individuals with unique gifts of discernment and insight.

Chance discovery while in pursuit of something else—and having the wit to recognize its importance—has occurred from time immemorial. From the discovery of quinine to floating soap, from the accidental production of penicillin to dynamite, humankind continues on in its inventive way, and sometimes serendipitously so in the footsteps of the three princes of Serendip.

PREFACE: JOHN L. HITCHCOCK
& STUART SHOTWELL

Plugging into the Worldfield

The Meaning of Synchronicity

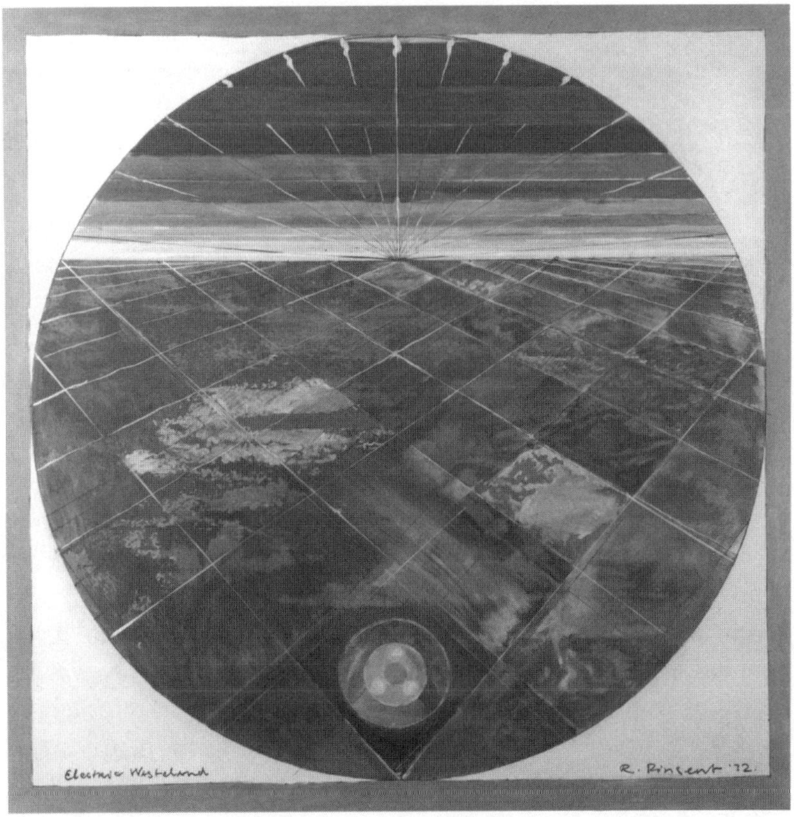

Richard Pinsent.
Electric Wasteland.
Oil on canvas,
45⅝×45¾, 1972.
Albright-Knox Art Gallery, Buffalo, New York. Gift of Seymour H. Knox, Jr., 1976.

Years ago I was at home preparing to go to a retreat center for a seminar—one that would give my life's work its direction, although beforehand I had no idea that such would be the case. As I was taking care of the usual mundane matters preparatory to a journey, there was suddenly a crash behind me in the next room. On investigating, I found that a fine Persian rug that had been hanging on the wall had fallen, though it had been in its place for over a year without incident. For someone else this might have been a trivial occurrence, but to me it was more than that, it was synchronicity in action. Though I sensed a meaning in the event, at the moment it happened I had no idea what the meaning could be. Yet as I continued on my way to and through the retreat, the meaning signaled by that simple happening became clear.

—JOHN L. HITCHCOCK

A CLASSIC INSTANCE OF SYNCHRONICITY is one that Jung himself liked to cite. One of his clients was discussing a dream of being given a golden scarab when a similar beetle suddenly flew against the consulting room window, tapping at it behind Jung's back. When Jung opened the window, the beetle flew in. Jung remarks:

> It was the nearest analogy to a golden scarab that one finds in our latitudes, a scarabaeid beetle *(Cetonia aurata),* which contrary to its usual habits had evidently felt an urge to get into a dark room at this particular moment. Nothing like it has ever happened to me before or since.[1]

In this example, it is plain to see that there was a connection between the beetle that entered the room and the beetle in the dream. The appearance of what we could call the "outer" beetle reinforced the significance of the "inner" beetle. To someone else it might seem merely a curious coincidence; but for the patient (and for Jung, who was capable of appreciating the patient's experience), the appearance of the "outer" beetle was charged with meaning.

On another memorable occasion, a teacher was explaining the concept of synchronicity to a group of students during a walk in the woods. "Imagine you were to bend down and scoop up a stone from the path at random," the teacher told them, "and when you looked at what you had picked up, you realized it was an arrowhead." As he spoke these words he accompanied them with the actions he was describing; and when he glanced at the stone he had picked up, he saw to his astonishment it was in fact an arrowhead. Again, there is a clear connection between inner and outer: the inner is the teacher's attempt to explain the concept of synchronicity; the "outer" is the discovery of the arrowhead.[2]

By its very nature, synchronicity has tremendous meaning to the one who experiences it, but often less to others. In the Persian rug incident, for example, the rug symbolized the past that was falling away as the author moved on. The outer event was not trivial: it was charged with the intense meaning of the inner event it signaled.

A key aspect of all instances of synchronicity is that they exhibit an *ordering* of events. (The term *synchronicity* is formed of two

Greek roots that mean "together–time," reflecting this simultaneous ordering.) The appearance of the beetle occurred in tandem with the telling of the client's dream; the arrowhead came to the teacher's hand as he uttered his explanation of the phenomenon; and the suspended carpet fell away in unison with the author's expectations of what his life was to be. The symbol in each case was the ordering factor: beetle, arrowhead, collapsing carpet. Yet despite this ordering of inner and outer events, neither inner nor outer causes the other. Thus Jung describes synchronicity as disclosing *acausal orderedness.* It is worth noting this aspect of synchronicity because we generally think of order as resulting from a chain of causes: B happens because of A, C because of B, and so forth. Events that are merely simultaneous—neither meaningful nor connected by cause and effect—cannot be said to be "ordered" at all: they merely happen without any linkage.

Another aspect of synchronicity is that it makes us feel that something larger than we are is trying to get our attention. It often occurs when we are in a heightened state—whether in love or despair, deep in thought, or deep in loneliness. It is at times like these, it seems (when we are most receptive to that something that is trying to reach us) that acausal orderedness is suddenly infused with meaning.

BUT DEFINING SYNCHRONICITY is the easy part. The difficult question—the *immediate* question in the mind of anyone who has experienced synchronicity, or who simply hears of it—is this: *How could the outer world be connected to our inner life?* In other words, what could the medium of such a connection possibly be? By "medium," we mean the thing that is in the middle, or that contains two things, so that a connection can occur between them. Air is a medium for sound; wire is a medium for electricity. Clearly, science as it is currently practiced rejects the possibility of any such medium between the outer world and our inner life. Yet there is a theory that explains this link between the two.

The theory holds that there is a higher reality than the outer world or the inner world, and it includes them both. It is thus called the *unitary reality.* The term Jung preferred was the *unus mundus,* Latin for "one-world." Another term for it is the *Worldfield.* This name evokes the vast fields of electromagnetic or gravitational forces that we know exist all around us; but the Worldfield is far vaster—is, in fact, all-inclusive.

This Worldfield is the medium that enfolds and connects the outer and inner, the material and the spiritual; it enables the connections we see in synchronicity to take place. There is no proof that the Worldfield exists; or at least none that will persuade scientists as readily as the action of a compass shows them that magnetic fields exist, or as readily as the action of orbiting planets convinces them that gravitation exists. Yet there are many phenomena within the purview of science that can only be explained if we accept the existence of the Worldfield. A simple example is the way the arms of a snowflake are formed. Its crystals form with exquisite symmetry, yet there is no way that the individual arms can "know" how the other arms are forming as the crystals leave the center and take shape, unless they take their pattern from the Worldfield. (For this very reason we sometimes use yet another name for the Worldfield: the Patterning.) In radioactive decay, as well, somehow the individual atoms in a piece of uranium each "know" when it is their turn to shed a particle—and know it so precisely that the decay of the entire sample over thousands of years can be predicted according to a mathematical formula. In theory the entire radioactive lump could shed all its particles in the first second or two and cease being radioactive; but in practice this does not happen because the Worldfield links the activity of all the atoms.

There are many other phenomena, too, of which science has evidence, but which some scientists intensely dislike acknowledging, in which the action of the Worldfield is quite obvious: these include parapsychological phenomena such as extrasensory perception (ESP).

HOW, THEN, DOES THE WORLDFIELD ACT ON US when we experience synchronicity? In answering this question, it is worth clarifying an essential point first. We tend to think of ourselves as part of the "outer" world, the world inhabited by the beetle, by the arrowhead, by the Persian carpet. But, this is not so. Rather, we dwell "in the middle," between the outer world and the inner world.

The outer world is the world of matter, the material world. The inner world (which is not truly "inside" us, but "inside" the material world) is the world of spirit, the spiritual world. Materialists argue that the spiritual world is only a figment of our hyperactive human imaginations and does not really exist, while others (for example, Buddhists and Christian Scientists) argue that the material world is an illusion, and only the spiritual is real. Most people will probably accept the reality of both the material and the spiritual to some degree or other.

Whether something we experience is material or spiritual, the only place in which we can experience it is within the psyche. The concept of psyche can be defined in various ways. In Greek it meant "soul" or "life," and it has been put to use in psychology to mean simply "the mind"—all the things that make up our mental activity.

The important point is that we have experiences that we classify as either spiritual or material, but we don't know spirit or matter *in themselves;* we only have experiences of them in our psyche. Jung (and others before him) pointed out that the ultimate nature of both spirit and matter cannot be represented—they transcend our ability to know them in themselves as they are. We can only know the psyche and what is in the psyche. Everything but the psyche comes to us through the medium of the psyche; and only the psyche, and what is in it, is known to us without any medium.[3]

So we can say that when we experience synchronicity, it is because the Worldfield "wants" the psyche to grasp the notion of a greater unity. It uses meaning to do so. It "breaks through" to our psyche by making an inner and outer event occur at the same time, and letting the psyche perceive the meaning of the connection. Synchronicity is a phenomenon in which the Worldfield provides two events—one outer and one inner—that get the attention of the psyche because they are ordered, but not linked by cause; and the psyche, to make sense of that acausal ordering, must invest those linked events with meaning.

Because the psyche is the place we experience the inner and outer worlds, that experience is always colored with our selves. In fact, we could say that we paint our environment, even the entire universe, with the colors of our selves and our ideas regarding the nature of things. This means that we can know our world only to the degree that we know ourselves; and also that by examining how we project our psyches on the world we can come to know our own deeper being. In doing so, we become more than simply aware of the world we are mirroring in our psyche; we become aware of ourselves.

Thus the realm of meaning is painted with the colors of the psyche, making it tantalizingly elusive and endlessly circular; but from that circularity arises the tremendous power of synchronicity to teach us about ourselves.

BUT THERE IS MORE TO BE SAID, specifically about meaning, before the full function of synchronicity will be clear. Picture the act of blowing across the mouth of a bottle to produce a tone. Making a tone in this way requires energy (the blowing) and a container (the bottle) for the sound waves that are produced as the air flows across the opening. The container provides for the reflection of the waves within it, and it enhances the waves in a way that depends on its size and shape. It may at first seem a humble comparison, but we suggest that synchronicity involves analogues of each of these aspects of producing a tone. The container is analogous to our consciousness (which is capable of "reflecting"), and the tones are analogous to the images of meaning that resonate within us.

As part of the evolution of the cosmos, consciousness has arisen as our tool for knowing, as well as for perceiving meaning. Since we tend to identify consciousness exclusively with our capacity for reason, it is important to remember that the reasoning intellect is only one of several faculties within consciousness. Other modes of knowing are largely nonrational. All that we know through memory images, our sense of ourselves as having continuity of being, and all forms of intuitive or extrasensory knowing are examples of nonrational knowing. Even some aspects of scientific discovery are of a nonrational nature, the whole realm of *dasein* outlined by Martin Heidegger, and certainly our sense of encounter with the divine are included as well.

It is also important to recognize that our consciousness functions by means of images. In the term *images* we can include not only visual pictures, but also emotions, sensations of touch, sounds, smells, perceptions of muscular function, pain, and even ideas.

If we ask whether you locked your door when you left home, or whether you need to buy more milk, a visual image comes to you of the door or the refrigerator, perhaps along with tactile images of turning the key or hefting the milk container when you had cereal or coffee this morning. Such images are linked in our minds in surprising ways. A common trick for remembering whether you have unplugged the iron or turned off the oven is to link the action with an anomalous image that you can recall more easily than the commonplace but critical action of pulling the plug from the wall or turning the oven control dial. The mother of an acquaintance says the name of one of the Mexican volcanoes, Popocatepetl, when she unplugs the iron. If she should wonder later whether she unplugged it, she usually will not remember the commonplace tactile image of doing so, but she can always remember the unusual auditory image of saying that foreign name.

Mental images, of whatever type, amount to energy transfers from wherever they are stored in your brain to the part or parts in which consciousness functions. Consciousness itself uses energy, as is clear from the fact that we cannot maintain our awareness without recharging it with both food and sleep. The images, then, are energy resonating in the consciousness.

A radio employs another resonance phenomenon—the resonance of radio waves in electrical circuits, which capture and focus the energy of the waves when the radio is tuned, just as the bottle captures and focuses the energy vibrations in the air. Similarly, the brain possesses *neural* circuits of many kinds. Some process visual stimuli, others tactile, and so on; the Papez circuit governs emotions. We could say that our experience of meaning involves a tuning of our neural circuits so that they can capture and focus the images resonating in our minds.

Taking this idea further, we can see that this "tuning in" to images occurs when we *match patterns* in our minds. This pattern-matching is at the heart of all human experience of meaning and metaphor. Here is an example: Ten years after one of the authors graduated from high school and left his hometown, he went back for a visit. Walking through the grounds of the county fair with a couple of his friends, they encountered a few others from their old class. Among them was a man who had been just a casual acquaintance. The author recognized him at once; but as they were all talking, he looked at the man's face, which had changed greatly in the previous decade and wondered *how* indeed he had recognized him. Then it became clear that on encountering him the author had actually seen that face *as he had known it ten years ago.* The implication of this fact is astonishing. In the author's view, his "I," i.e., his own consciousness, could not have recognized his old acquaintance at all, but something within him did recognize the man; it pulled out of the countless images in his memory just the right one and "superimposed" it over what his eyes were seeing. Or, to put it another way, his mind "tuned" itself so that the man's new image resonated with his old image. Suddenly this stranger "meant" the person the author had once known.

We could call this process *pattern resonance.* Something within us, which can be referred to as the "prime inhabitant," and which Jung referred to as the Self, is always on the lookout for possible pattern matches, or rather for resonance between images in our minds. Resonance between such images is what results in meaning.

Our very experience of meaning is often carried by language, which is a phenomenon that itself offers some instructive examples of pattern resonance. Language evokes meaning by creating images in our mind—objects, actions, attitudes, ideas, memories, and many other things—and it often works by using metaphor (the resonance of similar images). As a simple case, consider how many body parts are used in this manner, such as the head of the arrow we have already mentioned. Other examples are the *mouth* of the cave, the *foot* of a mountain or a *foot* of length, the *leg* of a stool, the *teeth* of a saw, and more abstract terms such as the *jaws* of death or the *eye* of a hurricane. Words link images; they provide a way for patterns to resonate in our minds.

As words, the names of individuals too are linked with both visual images and memories of events, resulting in a rich web of associations. So powerful are these associations that in a very real sense, a person's name means the person. Truly, names can be numinous—filled with a power beyond the natural or material. Thus a Native American proverb maintains that "when you name a thing, it *becomes.*"

Language is significant too because it is shared. Not only do we feel the flow of pattern-matching energy when we identify patterns and communicate in words, but we grasp the universality of the experience of meaning: what we know, others can know, or at least can know within the limits imposed by the variations in our psyches.

WHAT ELSE CAN WE KNOW OR GUESS about the Worldfield? For one thing, we can surmise that it possesses cosmic dimensions because it links the meanings of separate and distinct happenings.

Researcher Louisa Rhine has collected and related hundreds of well-documented examples of extrasensory perception, including the case of a woman whose mother's car was stolen. Two nights later the woman dreamed of a certain street fifteen miles away in a nearby city where the car would be found. She told her mother and husband about the dream and then drove to the place, finding the car without further difficulty. As if that were not striking enough, when she asked the people in the area about the car, she was told it had not been parked there until a few minutes before she arrived.[4]

A woman in California was frightened briefly by an intruder in her back yard. Minutes later her husband, who was on an island in the Caribbean, called to ask why she was disturbed. Even thousands of miles away, he had felt her distress.

Not all cases of ESP link loved ones and family; many involve information that relates to perfect strangers. It is as if there is a center of all things that functions as a clearinghouse of meaning, matching the patterns or images of everything that is going on in a general area of time and space, and linking them to individual psyches that are open to receive the meaning. This center seems able to function via concrete objects such as the stolen car, the arrowhead, or symbols printed on Tarot cards or written on paper. It can also function through less concrete means: the spoken words of prayers, the physical condition of one's body, or a general cultural atmosphere, as in the receptivity of groups to ideas. In short, it can function via anything physical or spiritual, and bring the meaning to consciousness in individual psyches through dreams, ESP, and synchronicity alike.

IN VIEW OF THE APPARENTLY UNIVERSAL LINKAGE of spirit and matter, it seems that one function of the Worldfield is to increase the consciousness of meaning over all the living earth. Its tool to this end is something we can call "formativity," following psychologist Erich Neumann.[5]

We can best explain this concept by sketching how the universe "works." The cosmos originated as a ball of flowing energy. Initially, the energy interacted with itself, precipitating pairs of particles with equal and opposite properties, so that the net increase of any property was zero. Even the energy that did this was balanced by negative energy in the form of gravity that held it all together, so that the sum there was zero as well. Yet the particles produced also possessed patterning and, together with others, brought forth all of the forms that we observe in the universe, or might observe if we could be everywhere at once and remain for all of time. The universe, in short, is the result of a kind of divine play at the generation of forms. So the universe does not really "work"; it "plays." This play at making forms is what Neumann calls formativity.

The Worldfield, then, plays at matching patterns for us. Its formativity is endlessly rich and fertile; we need only be alive and awake to it. This image of divine play also suggests the freedom of creation, for the number of forms that can be realized is apparently infinite.

A clue to this infinity can be seen in the fact that all visible forms in the universe are ultimately derived from the simplest element, hydrogen, inasmuch as there was a moment in creation when the newborn cosmos was virtually pure hydrogen. In that moment, the infinite potential of formation was concentrated in the simplest material form. In a very real sense, everything that exists now was once one. Thus what is deepest (farthest back) in creation is also the simplest of all things. We should be alert to the possibility that the metaphoric structures, or symbols, through which we perceive meaning may ultimately be very few in number, reflecting that deep and ancient simplicity.

Consider for example, the mandala formed by a circle that is divided into four parts by a cross. Such a mandala is an apt symbol for the wholeness of the universe (the circle) into which everything fits (the arms of the cross). As a four-chambered organ, our heart is also like this mandala, and through the resonance of patterns, the mandala becomes the heart of the universe.

Because of this simple similarity of patterns in the universe, each meaning-experience we have, whether in synchronicity or dreams or ESP, renews our sense of the infinite depth of reality. That is why something as simple as a found stone or a flying beetle or a fallen carpet can be the link that puts us deeply in touch with something far more significant.

But synchronicity reveals more than this, still more. It suggests that there is a continual internalization of the formative, i.e., creative, process itself in beings such as ourselves, so that the experience of meaning not only reveals the depth of creation, it also, in time, penetrates us more deeply, revealing to us a greater potential creative depth within. The creative process also opens us, which is to say that it simplifies us into our essential form, linking us more deeply to the creative reality itself.

What sometimes baffles us when we are linked with that creative reality, that Worldfield at play, is that the Worldfield itself is without form, though it constantly creates form in the universe. We may draw on the Worldfield's creativity to create forms for it (the Ancient of Days, the Whirlwind), names (Jehovah, Allah, the Father-Mother), and images (whether a crude statuette in a cave or the splendid icons of the Orthodox faith), but it forever transcends our creativity—and its own.[6]

EVERY TIME WE EXPERIENCE MEANING IN SYNCHRONICITY, our sense of wonder at the meaning of the universe is jostled awake. We ask ourselves, What does this meaning *mean*? The answer to this question is that the Worldfield, or if you prefer, God, is bringing forth the ultimate unity of all things through the experience of meaning.

As divine energy flows into all the containers with which it can resonate, the music of the universe is created. This is God blowing across the mouths of all the bottles at once. When the container is sufficiently complex that reflection becomes self-reflectivity, we can finally realize that we ourselves are the notes of the cosmic symphony.

Notes

1. Synchronicity is the term used by C. G. Jung to refer to the meaningful connection of an "outer" event with an "inner" state, in which causality can be ruled out. Although it is often confused with a similar concept, serendipity, the two are distinct. Serendipity is finding something valuable or agreeable without specifically seeking for it; there is no meaningful connection between outer event and inner state implied in the term. The distinction is significant. (Carl Gustav Jung, *The Structure and Dynamics of the Psyche,* 2d ed., Princeton University Press, 1969. *The Collected Works of C.G. Jung,* v. 8, paragraph 843. It is customary to refer to these works by paragraph number and not by page. *The Collected Works* are number XX in the Bollingen Series.)
2. By the way, this example demonstrates the difference between synchronicity and serendipity. If the teacher had not been talking about picking up an arrowhead, and

had happened to pick one up, that would have been mere serendipity. But the fact that he was talking about picking up an arrowhead made his picking one up more than just a pleasantly surprising happenstance: it gave meaning to the event.

3. As Jung put it: "Matter and spirit both appear in the psychic realm as distinctive qualities of conscious contents. The ultimate nature of both is transcendental, that is, irrepresentable, since the psyche and its contents are the only reality which is given to us without a medium" (Carl Gustav Jung, *The Structure and Dynamics of the Psyche,* 2d ed., Princeton University Press, 1969. *The Collected Works of C.G. Jung,* v. 8, paragraph 420). This is why, incidentally, our view of reality is so flexible: we experience it in our psyche. Human psyches three hundred years ago saw the cosmos in Newtonian terms; today they may see it in terms of post-Einsteinian physics. We periodically revamp our thinking about the material world when we find a metaphor (and theories like those of Newton, Einstein, and other physicists are essentially metaphors) that fits the outer world better, explaining more of its phenomena. Hopefully, we can make the same progression in our understanding of the world of spirit.
4. Louisa E. Rhine. *ESP in Life and Lab: Tracing Hidden Channels.* New York: Macmillan, 1967, pp. 99–100.
5. As Neumann puts it, "In individuation and in the creative process alike, it now becomes clear that the center of the creative and formative process is a reality which is itself formless. . . . Analogous to this is the affirmation of the formlessness of the divine as a creative reality which, though itself a continuously form-making agency, is not to be worshiped under any particular form or image because. . . . it always remains superior to its own creative and formative potency." (Erich Neumann. *The Place of Creation.* Tr. Hildegard Nagel et. al. Bollingen Series LX13. Princeton University Press, 1989, p. 370.

JOHN L. HITCHCOCK's observations and researches provided the basis for this article; this particular formulation of his ideas developed in an authorial conversation between Hitchcock and his friend STUART SHOTWELL. Hitchcock holds masters' degrees in astronomy and clinical mental health counseling, as well as a doctorate in the phenomenology of science and religion. He is the author of four books in the latter field as well as a practicing clinical mental health counselor. Shotwell holds a doctorate in classical philology and is currently the managing editor of the Swedenborg Foundation's new translation series of Swedenborg's theological works originally written in Latin. Shotwell's publications include a volume of short stories and the forthcoming translation of Emanuel Swedenborg's *Worship and Love of God.*

Chances Are . . .

PROVIDENCE? SERENDIPITY? OR FATE?

PART I

Life or Death?

first near frost,
morning glories
now a deeper blue,
their white veins
now stripes of crimson
—Art Stein

. . . In every instance
where God seems blind and uncaring,
we fail to see the real form of things
from our limited perspective in this world.
Were we able to see the eternal uses,
we might, like God, permit evil.
This does not make evil good;
but despite all our efforts
to stand against events we do not choose,
we might notice what deeply ingrained tendencies
are being built into us.
This can combine with the love of life
[our inmost ruling love] to create our eternal use.
—Wilson Van Dusen
The Design of Existence

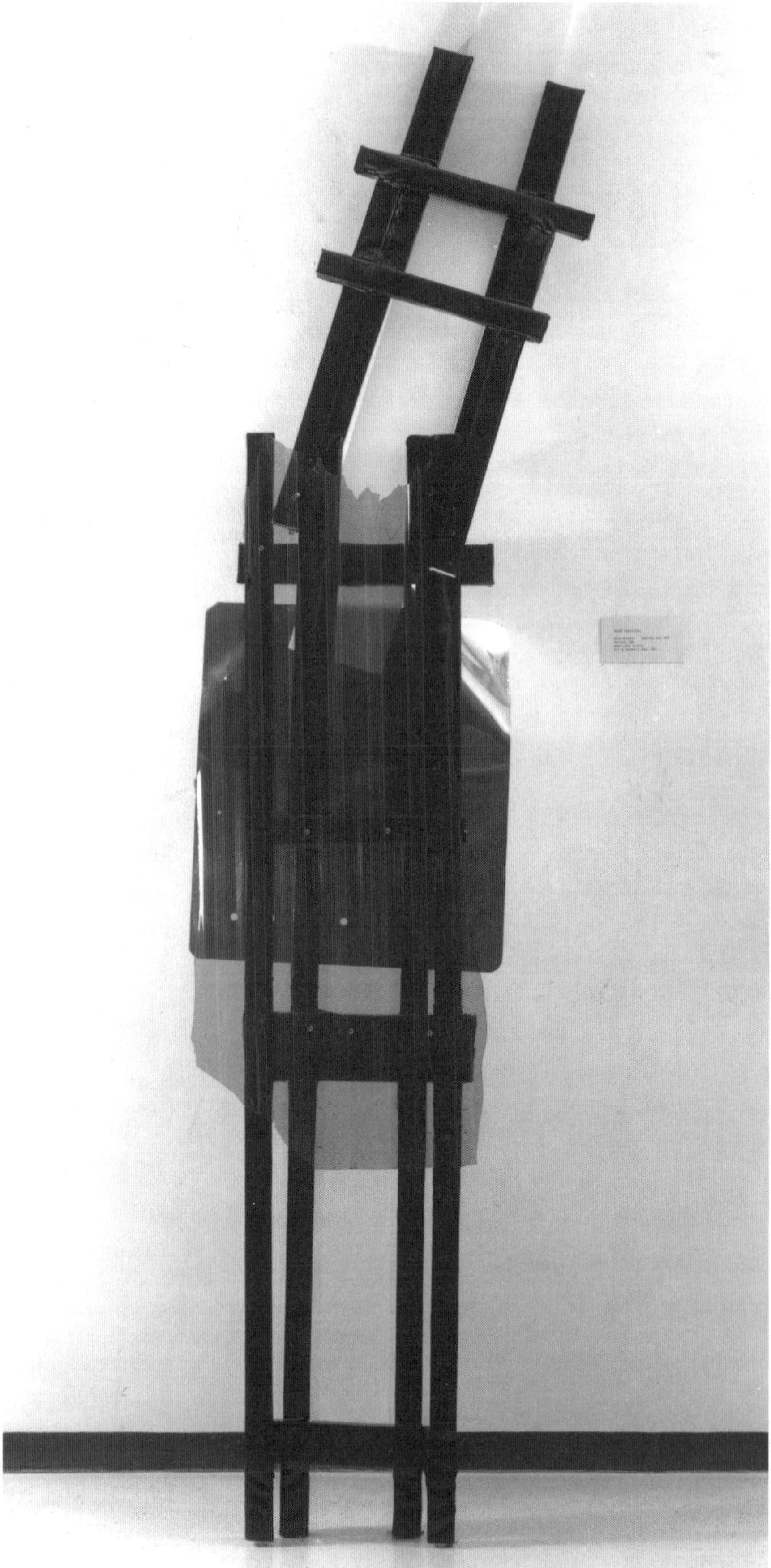

David Hatchett. *Untitled.* Wood, vinyl, and plastic, 108×24×5 inches, 1982. Albright-Knox Art Gallery, Buffalo, New York. Gift of Seymour H. Knox, Jr., 1983.

JOE LUNIEVICZ

Fallout

The sky is falling.

I look out my window, and the sky is falling in large pieces of steel, concrete, paper, blood, and bone.

IT'S OCTOBER 11TH, 2001, thirty days since my office was destroyed on the sixteenth floor of the World Trade Center, Tower Two. I stand on 23rd Street and 6th Avenue, looking up at the new office building we've just moved into. I squint because the glare from the skyscrapers around me is intense.

I watch as a plane comes out of the sky and hits it.

I watch it again and again before I blink my eyes and the sky clears. I step through the front doors and into the elevators.

We've been bombing the Taliban in Afghanistan for five days. My stomach still turns to jelly when I'm outside and a loud noise assaults me—when a car hits a large pot-hole, a siren blares, or a garbage truck releases a metal container that crashes to the earth. I resist the urge to duck, but inside I flinch. My exterior is molded plastic, hard to the touch. It's easier to exist indoors where the noises are muffled.

The critical-incident counselor called these images intrusive thoughts. Intrusive, as if they intrude upon a tranquil place. Inside my head, if tranquility exists, it lies behind a door, far back in the dark.

ON TUESDAY, SEPTEMBER 11TH I arrive at work at 8:25 AM, early because I'm training a four-day course called "Community HIV/AIDS Education," and I like to get in before most of the participants do. I work at a behavioral and social sciences research and training not-for-profit, specializing in AIDS and Substance Abuse Issues. I get in early because it helps to settle my nerves before I have to get up in front of an audience.

I pass Melvin, our logistics coordinator, in the hall. He has already set up the training room with participant manuals at each chair and pencils for their pre-test questionnaires.

"Goin' for a smoke," he says. He's a black man in his late fifties, with a heart condition that has recently flared up and left him sallow-faced, hunched over, and tired. He has been back on the job for only a month since his stay in the hospital.

Mary, my co-trainer, comes in as Melvin walks out, and they say hello as they pass. We've been co-training together for over eight years. Some twenty-one years ago Mary recruited me for the United States Peace Corps—only we didn't know each other then.

We sit next to my desk. My desktop is covered with training contract folders—color-coded green and yellow. My in-box is overflowing. My computer warms up and prompts me for a user password. A picture of my wife, Karen, stares back at me smiling from a street in San Francisco. "Keep that picture," she told me once. "It's the one that makes me look thin." My window faces Tower One, and I turn my back to it so I can talk with Mary. We make small talk the way two colleagues, nervous before their presentations begin, do. Mary makes me laugh. She and I always laugh when we train together. My hand shakes while I laugh, so I set my almond steamed milk down on my desk so I don't spill it. It's a coffee substitute for an anxious stomach. Then I hear what I think is thunder and look up as a flash of light fills the room.

Lightning, I think, outside my window behind me. "I didn't know we were supposed to have a thunderstorm today," I say and turn around to look out the window.

IT'S OCTOBER 12TH. At acting class a friend says, "Oh, you were only on the sixteenth floor. That's not that high up." He seemed almost disappointed in me. I guess compared to those who were killed on the ninety-fifth floor, he is right. Still, inside, my gut twists. Outside I smile and nod. "You're right," I say, "I was lucky."

OUTSIDE MY WINDOW THE SKY IS FALLING. I see paper and large objects, indistinguishable objects, fall. They whistle as they descend like flame-tailed comets. I hear the sound of glass shrieking as it cuts through the air.

Outside the Trade Center Melvin, a lit cigarette dangling from his lip, trailing a smoke lariat, looks up and sees the whole thing. The plane appears from nowhere and disappears into the side of the building. The explosion rocks him backwards into the black metal fence that rings the graveyard at Trinity Church.

"Did you see that?" he asks a man who passes by. The man ignores him. He has headphones on, a gray suit, and a pink tie. "Did you see that plane hit the tower?" he asks another, but nobody stops and nobody listens. He stands and stares up at the smoke and the flames and wonders if he's imagining it all.

"IT'S A BOMB," I say to myself and then a voice inside my head says, *Get away from the windows and find an arch.* The 'arch' is a holdover from my grade-school days when I was taught to hide under an arch during a bomb drill because arches are the strongest structural part of a building. The pieces of falling sky are so close they make my skin crawl, so I jump out of my chair and move away from the window. "Get away from the windows and get under an arch," I say. My voice is calm even though adrenaline is flowing; my heart is pounding and my fingers tingle as if the skin is stretched and ready to burst.

Mary and three participants from the training room stand nearby, crowded into the hall outside my office in the training corridor. There are three—Stanley, a woman reverend, and someone else whose face is hidden by the door. "Take them to the stairway by the elevator and wait there," I tell Mary. "Leave your bags. Just go." She nods and moves. They disappear into the center of the building.

I go the other way to see if anyone else on my side of the building knows what is going on. I look out my boss's window, eight offices down the hall, and see the wound in the side of Tower One. It is black, its edges blurred by billowing gray smoke and flames that flicker from beneath the darkness. I stare at it, unable to move.

I see Bob, our operations manager, and John, a researcher, and tell them, "We have to get out of here. There's a hole in Tower One, and it looks pretty bad. Let's get everyone out." I talk over Bob. I don't know what he is saying, but he stops talking, and both he and John nod.

I see Mary over by the stairs. "Take them down," I say. I catch a glimpse of the stairs as they open the door and see how crowded they are—packed but moving. We stand there a moment watching people move past us in a steady steam. I hear feet tapping the stairs and heavy breathing. Then the door closes, and it's silent again. "Let's check the floor for others," I say.

"Right," John says. "I'll check the left side." His eyes are wide open, and he's breathing fast. I wonder if I look the same.

"I'll take the right," I say. We head off in different directions.

The first door I knock on opens. Andy, the head of a research program, stands looking at me, his eyes unfocused as if he's been lost in thought.

"We've got to get off the floor," I say.

"What?" he says, still not fully present.

"This is not a drill. This is serious. It's an emergency. Stop what you're doing and get out."

He looks at me for a second, then his eyes focus, and he nods. I go past Bruce's office and walk past Hilary's, shouting, "This is an emergency. This is the real thing. Everybody get to the emergency station by the elevators." I knock on closed doors, then stop and think, *Hilary always keeps his door and shades closed so maybe he didn't hear me knock.* And because he's a friend, I go back to his door and open it. His office is empty. *Make sure nobody's hidden behind their doors,* I think, *because researchers are like that. They'll hide and ignore.* I go back and open all the closed doors.

A researcher steps out of one of the inner, windowless offices. "What's going on?" he asks.

"Get to the emergency station," I say. "This is not a drill. Everybody has to get off the floor." In my head I sound like the Russian submarine captain in the movie *The Russians Are Coming, The Russians Are Coming* when he shouts in a thick Russian accent, "Emergency, everybody to get from street."

A woman steps out of her office.

"Get off the floor. This is no bullshit. Everybody off the floor."

She looks at me, her hands aggressively on her hips, her face etched with annoyance—but she moves and I go on checking the rest of the offices.

John comes up behind me, and we head back to the stairs. The floor is clear. Bob is sending people down the stairs when we get there.

"Has anyone checked the bathrooms?" Bob asks.

"No," John says and runs to the men's room.

I run back to the window to see what else has happened to Tower One. The hole seems larger, its lips swelling. The sky is littered with floating pieces of paper like giant confetti. There is an acrid smell in the air. I have a phantom sense of smell from a nose that's been broken ten times on the rugby pitch, so I know the odor must be thick for it to penetrate my nasal passages. When I return to the stairs, John says the bathrooms are clear.

"Go," I say. "I'll be right behind you." I run back to my office to get my wallet, palm pilot, keys, and book. Since I was a kid I've always carried a book with me as a kind of security blanket. I know I want to have ID on me if something happens, and I either get killed or have to prove who I am to police. I'd spent two-and-a-half years in Honduras as a Peace Corps Volunteer, some of it during periods of martial law, so I know the value of carrying identification. Also, my brother was murdered twelve years ago, and without identification his body lay in the morgue for almost four weeks. I don't think twice about my fencing equipment—competitive gear I've been collecting and using since I was nineteen. The bag is four feet tall, a few feet wide, and weighs near forty pounds. It stays.

As soon as I return to the stairs the intercom comes to life for the first time and a voice rings out, "There is a fire in Tower One. Tower Two is not in danger. I repeat, Tower Two is not in danger. Stay in your offices and stay on your floor."

Rich, from accounting, and I look at each other. "Let's get out of here," I say. Two women from accounting come out of opening elevator doors. I stare at them in disbelief. They laugh like they are in on some private joke and run past me to their offices.

"We're getting our bags and purses," they say as they pass.

I stare at them, then run back to the windows one more time. When I return they are gone. Rich and I are the only ones still on the floor. I wonder if all are truly out. I wonder if we missed somebody.

"Let's go," I say.

"I'm going to stay," he says.

I look at him. "Are you sure?" I ask.

"Yes," he says.

I hesitate another second. It is a weird moment in time. I'm not really sure if there is anything else I should do. I fight the urge to run, look left then right, then hit the stairs.

MARY WAITS FOR ME on the mezzanine of Tower Two where the stairs let her out. Revolving glass doors behind her open out onto the courtyard where the summer concerts take place. The chairs and bandstand are crushed beneath debris that continues to fall. Police and security block the doors. In front of her escalators lead down to the mall level, taking people to safety.

"Do you think we'll have the training today?" a participant asks her.

"I don't think so," she says, "but I'm sure we'll be able to pick it up tomorrow."

John finds her there a few moments later, and they wait for me together. People shout as they come out of the stairs and see the sky falling. Everybody ducks as if the pieces are going to come through the glass that surrounds the mezzanine. Security tells them loudly to head downstairs and out into the mall.

IT IS NOT AS CROWDED ON THE STAIRS as when I saw Mary go down, but there are still plenty of people walking down. I can't count them because I can only see one floor up and one floor down. I concentrate on the floor below me. I see a pair of black, women's shoes, with two-inch lifts discarded on the side of one of the platforms between floors. Two heavy women are in front of me. Their slow pace holds me up, along with those behind me. One of the women is heavy and limps slightly because of her weight. I stop myself from getting too close to them, from pushing them out of the way. Young men come down fast behind me, and I feel them close at my back, breathing hard. I think, *Why can't one of these women get in front of the other so others can go past?* and then, *People behind us had better slow down or this is going to be a Who Concert.* After three flights of stairs the two women finally step aside. We bolt past them. I resist the urge to yell, "Slow down," and "Don't panic." Fear builds up inside of me like an animal trying to claw its way out of my stomach. We reach a peak velocity together and just keep going down, one notch below panic. I don't know what happens to the two heavy women. I don't see them again. I beat the stairs with the soles of my feet and turn and turn as we reach each new successive landing. The numbers on the exit doors get lower and lower.

A door is open in front of me and I step out into daylight filtered through the glass that surrounds the mezzanine level of Tower Two. I'm dizzy, and my head is spinning. I see the courtyard. It is like Charlton Heston's New York City in the movie *The Omega Man*—rubble covered by white dust. I stop with my mouth hanging open and wonder, for the first time, if there are bodies out there and if people have fallen. I don't want to see bodies, but I look anyway. I have to.

Security and police yell at us to get to the escalator, "Move it. Move it," they say.

I'm still looking outside when another explosion shakes the building. The floor seems to move beneath me. I can't hear anything for a moment. Small particles of dust float down from the ceiling like snow. Everything moves in slow motion.

OUTSIDE MELVIN SEES THE SECOND PLANE HIT OUR TOWER and is knocked down by the concussion. A woman and her child are knocked down in front of him, and he helps them up, then places them behind him. People run past them either down into the subway or out, away from the Trade Center.

"Let's get out of here," Melvin says and shepherds them toward City Hall.

Mary and John step outside the exit near Sam Goody's onto Liberty Street as the second explosion hits. A man on the street in front of them is pierced by a falling piece of steel. They turn around quickly and go back into the building. They run across the mall toward Borders and go upstairs to the surface again. They huddle outside with others beneath the overhang of the building, across from the graveyard where Melvin had just stood. Debris continues to fall from above. Someone in authority tells them to stay beneath the cover of the building. But Mary and John take off, not waiting and not looking behind them. They head uptown, toward City Hall.

People are yelling and running toward the escalator, pushing past me. I start to move and then, once moving can't seem to slow myself down. I'm running by the time I reach the escalator.

"Move it! Move it! Move it!" men in uniform yell. They wave and point downstairs. My feet touch the escalator's steel and carry me three or four steps until I come up to a man who is stationary, letting the stairs take him down. He is straightening his suit jacket, adjusting his tie. His presence calms me and makes me stop. I walk past him with measured steps, in control of my body again, and follow the others to the revolving doors that lead to the mall.

Security yells, "Get out! Get out! Everybody get out!" and people run. I watch a man run into the revolving doors and push through them quickly. I follow him. They hiss as they spin, and I emerge into the mall. White dust floats down, settling on top of us. More security people yell at us to run and head toward the E-train subway platform. I stop near Victoria's Secret and the street exit by Sam Goody.

A security man says, "You can't go out there" and waves me away.

"I know. I just want to see," I say. I stand there a second and watch as a large piece of building hits the ground outside the doors, some fifty yards away. I run a little and then slow to a fast walk. No one is panicking. Everyone is hurrying, but no one is knocking anyone down or out of the way. I figure the E-train is the best place to be—underground, like in a bomb shelter. I then think, *If I have to, I can walk out to Chambers Street that way, underground, because the tunnel is so long.* But I reach the E-train platform and see a train sitting there. The image is surreal. People are packed in the first two cars, just like they are during rush hour, arms and legs spilling out of the doorways, black briefcases and backpacks protruding like small tumors. No one is in the third car or the other cars forward. I debate getting on and decide not to. I walk forward because it seems too easy to just get on and leave the area and that worries me. I think, *What if there is something else I can do?* and, *Is the subway train the safest place to be right now? What if the doors close and the train stays put and we all get stuck?* Then I remember the E-train goes away from the World Trade Center—up town. It's the last stop south on the E-line. I walk to the head of the train. I see Dave, an accountant from my organization, walking ahead of me. I want to call his name, but I don't. As he steps on the train, he turns back and sees me. We smile at each other, and I step on just as the alarm rings for 'all aboard.'

The train pulls out.

I walk over to him, and we shake hands.

Another man stands next to us. He says there has been a second plane.

"What plane?" I ask.

"I saw two people jump out of Tower One and fall to the ground," he says. "It was horrible." We stand and stare at each other for a while. I get off at the 14th Street and 8th Avenue station because I have to call Karen and let her know I am okay. Dave nods, and we say goodbye as the doors close behind me, and the train pulls out. I figure 14th Street should be far enough away from the Trade Center to be safe.

Only I can't find a phone that works at the station. So I exit and head for the surface. I walk over to Sixth Avenue because the E-train might stop service soon and, I think, *The F train doesn't go under the Trade Center so it will still be running.*

When I get to Sixth Avenue and 14th Street, I see the towers and the two black holes, and the smoke. I stare, and my body shakes a little.

Three young girls laugh, and point, and I yell at them, "It's not funny. People died up there. They're dying up there. It's not funny."

I go down into the 14th Street 6th Avenue station, pass through the turnstiles, and find a phone that works. I wait in line behind three other people, then call Karen. She doesn't answer, so I leave a message, "I'm okay," say goodbye, and hang up. It's just past 9:30 AM. I sit down against the wall and wait for an F-train to appear. Ten minutes later it arrives. The tracks take me home to Queens.

Karen is two months pregnant, and, as I ride the train, I worry that she will lose the baby. The longer the ride takes, the more I worry.

"This is Roosevelt Station," the loudspeaker announces, and I step off the car onto the platform.

I run the three blocks home.

Karen is at the door, crying.

"I'm okay," I say as we hold each other. "There was a train waiting for me. It's as if it was waiting just for me."

"Your father called and . . ." she begins but I don't hear what she is saying.

On the television Tower Two is collapsing. It is a replay, and it is being shown again and again and again. I sink to my knees on the living room floor and don't move. I can't stop staring at the screen.

Then Tower One collapses.

MELVIN WALKS HOME TO BROOKLYN. Mary walks two and a half miles to Grand Central Station and eventually takes Metro North home to Westchester. A man covered with ash and blood sits near her, staring out the window, crying.

THE SKY IS FALLING. It's October 13th. Friends still touch me and hug me and say, "Thank God," when they see me.

People stop what they're doing when they find out I was on the sixteenth floor. "You were there?" they say. "In the Tower?"

In Pennsylvania at a reading of a short story of mine that has just been published, a whole room grows quiet when someone announces that I was in Tower Two. I feel their gazes like nervous hands laid upon my skin.

ON SEPTEMBER 17TH our whole agency meets at Beth Israel Hospital. We touch each other to make sure our skin is real. A critical-incident counselor talks to us about the psychological process of dealing with trauma. He says we may get intrusive thoughts and a spectrum of feelings running from guilt and shame to jubilation. He tells us about the thirty-day rule. "If you've still got things cooking after thirty days then . . . well, that's something to worry about." He says this with a look of both concern and despair etched into his face.

Our executive director calls several of us heroes.

Andy comes up to me and says, "I guess I should thank you for saving my life." I nod and smile. I do not feel like a hero.

All are present and accounted for from our floor. No one is missing.

IT IS OCTOBER 26TH, 2001. The fire station on 18th Street, like all the fire stations in Manhattan, has a memorial in front of it. I pass it today as I go to lunch.

Daydreaming at work later, I picture the men in uniform—security, police, and fire department—standing by the escalator, shouting, "Move it! Move it! Move it!" I'm sure they are dead. I'm sure they stayed as long as people were still coming down out of those stairs and into the light of the mezzanine.

Why was a train waiting for me and nothing was waiting for them? When all is said and done, my leaving was easy. How could I look upon it as anything but easy? That is why I hesitated on the 16th floor. That is why I hesitated before I stepped onto the subway car. I asked myself, "Isn't there something else I can do?"

"Your job was to come home to me," my wife says. "Your job was to come home to us."

JOE LUNIEVICZ has had literary fiction published in both national and regional publications, including *Smoke, Aberrations, 96INC., Amelia, Dragon Magazine,* and *Another Chicago Magazine.* His nonfiction has appeared in *Body Positive* and *Rugby* (where he wrote the "Zen Rugger" column). He is also a playwright and lives in New York City.

GREGORY KIMURA

To Daniel Pearl

(kidnapped and killed in Pakistan)

My thirteen-year-old daughter writes a story
    for her English class that is due tomorrow:
    "What Ever Happened to . . ."
Proud of her story,
she tells me it is about you, Daniel.
I flinch and wince uncomfortably.
"What's wrong, Dad?" she says.
I cringe, founder, "It's just, it's so . . . shocking . . ."

Like me, Daniel, you are a writer,
but you are snatched from the streets of Karachi
where you went to find the truth.
I would be there too if that were my truth to find,
but my truths are closer to my home and my family.
It is you who are taken hostage by deluded men
    twisted by hate,
you who are stolen from your beautiful wife and unborn child.
Now I can only grow sad and stammer
    at my child's excitement.

Later, I find her in bed weeping, her story,
handwritten in red ink, torn to pieces on her desk.
"Why?" I ask.
Sobbing she says, "I don't want to write something
    shocking . . ."

The story lay upon the kitchen table,
pieces of paper, torn and stained with red ink.

We study the pieces under a bright lamp, my wife and I.
Then we get to work. Matching, assembling, and taping
together shattered bits and fragments.
In a few hours it is reassembled—
the way I wish we could reassemble you, Daniel.
I wish we could take your broken body torn to pieces
by confused men and put it back together with tape
    and computer.
We can't, but I saved your story.
In it you lived.
And now, my friend, you will always live.

After seven glorious years in six different colleges and universities, GREGORY KIMURA received his bachelor of arts degree in creative writing from Sierra Nevada College. By day, he is a Silicon Valley technical writer, by night a poet. This is his first published poem.

DONNA MASSIE OWNBY

No Rats in Heaven

Paul Klee. *Tomcat's Turf.* Watercolor, gouache, and oil on gesso on two sections of cloth mounted on light cardboard, 1919. The Metropolitan Museum of Art, New York. The Berggruen Klee Collection, 1984.

THE NEW MORNING SUN was slanting through the window and over the rose-colored linoleum on the bedroom floor. Eyes half-closed, Isla June awoke to the sounds of the morning in the old farmhouse. She could hear the groan of the black iron frying pan as it slid across the top of Mama's cook stove. Then the fatback began to pop and sizzle in the pan. Like every morning Mama was up early to start the day and the fire in the old wood cook stove. Isla felt warm and safe inside the old house, her young life sheltered from the outside world, taken up with carefree days and work on the farm. Her nights filled with whippoorwill songs and the orchestra of night creatures. She stuck her head out from under the patchwork quilt and listened to Papa and Mama talking about Jack. Jack was Papa's small black-and-white dog, still asleep in the old shoebox under the bed.

Mama had used the same shoebox last spring to hatch her chickens. Seemed to Isla, her Mama had a knack for hatching chickens. She would turn the eggs carefully each day and keep them warm in the shoebox under the bed. Finally the raucous peeping would begin. That was always exciting for Isla and Mattie Rose. They were used to new life arriving on the farm, but the transformation of eggs into baby chicks was always special.

Isla could hear Papa talking about Jack, about he was too old to do the job anymore. Isla wondered if Jack could hear him, too. Jack had been sleeping under the bed much of the time lately. Papa said he knew just how Jack felt. Jack had been with Papa a long time. No one really knew how old he was. Jack had just shown up one day, and Papa kept him. Mama said God gave him to Papa, as Papa was feeling down on account of the dry spell.

Isla woke up Mattie Rose sleeping beside her. A small face turned up, out from under the quilt and said, "What did you poke me for? I was getting up." Isla didn't answer but slipped out of bed, her bare feet hit the cold, rose linoleum. Chilled, she ran into the kitchen and stood near the big, white cook stove. Jack slowly followed behind and lay down under it. The old stove had warmed the family for many years. It was a friend. Isla could close her eyes and smell the sweet-butter pound cake, which would come from its oven on special occasions. The screech of the hinges on the oven door would summon the children to the kitchen in anticipation of a slice of soft, warm cake. Mama's hot bread was good, too.

Johnny was already sitting at the table drinking a glass of milk and eating one of Mama's biscuits. Mattie Rose slipped into the chair beside Isla still pushing the curly brown hair from her face, and said, "What's wrong with Jack?"

Papa said, "Nothing is wrong with Jack. Don't you worry." Papa went on talking to Mama. "I was counting on those hams to pay for the younguns' shoes this year. If varmints get them, I don't know what we'll do." New shoes; Isla was off in a daydream. She envisioned herself sitting on the front bench at church. When people passed she stuck out her feet so they could see her shiny new shoes. Everyone would notice her. Friends would look at her and wish they had new shoes, too. It would be a perfect Sunday.

Just then a swift kick under the old claw-foot table woke her from her daydream. Johnny was good at that. She thought, boys must never have daydreams, and they didn't want anyone else to have one either. Isla began to think, if Jack couldn't hunt the rats anymore, she would never get her new shoes. Papa had left the house that morning with Jack following behind him. You never saw one without the other, though it was getting harder and harder for Jack to keep up.

Living on the farm, Isla had seen new life come and old life go, new spring corn green in the fields, and by fall brown flags flying. Papa said everything had a purpose and a season. But that winter day Papa returned from the barn without Jack, and all Isla knew of life and its purpose seemed far away. Afterwards, Papa would never talk about it; all he would say was that was between him, Jack, and the angels. Isla knew Papa had not been able to watch Jack suffer anymore, but she would never ask Papa.

Isla thought she never wanted a pair of new shoes again; she just wanted to see Jack following behind Papa. She supposed they may get another dog, but it would never be the same without Jack. That night Papa put his gun back in the corner and went off to bed early. Isla could hear Mattie Rose quietly sobbing and then falling asleep beside her.

Deep into the night Isla heard Jack's little squeaky bark. A chase was on. He ran through the barn lot as fast as a deer, his little black-and-white coat glistening, eyes and nose wet with excitement of the chase. He could run and jump so high. Isla couldn't wait to wake up Papa and tell him Jack was well and home again. She awoke to the moonlight, and her blonde hair fell over the side of the bed as her eyes peered into the old shoebox, but Jack was not there. She rubbed her eyes and looked again. He wasn't there. In that moment she knew Jack would never return to the shoebox. She also knew from now on there would be no rats in heaven.

DONNA MASSIE OWNBY lives with her husband on a working goat and cattle farm in Virginia. The farm is home to four generations of Ownbys, the children of the red deer, and many other forms of wildlife. Donna began to write stories as a young girl when she listened to her Papa play the banjo and tell his own stories. Sometimes stories about angels. Donna believes angels are sent to those who need comforting.

SYLVIA M. SHAW

The Coffin

LURLINE PETTIGREW STIRRED COMFORTABLY IN HER SLEEP, unaware that under her bed, hidden behind the dust ruffle, slept a large new coffin. The scent of polished mahogany should have alerted her; the glow of the brass handles should have drawn her to her knees to look under the high bed frame. But when she awoke, she sprang to her feet with an energy at odds with her gray hair and moved past the coffin, oblivious to it for a fifth day in a row. She hurried into the morning. None of the inconveniences of the revolution had slowed her down. Not that there was anything that pressing to do; it was simply her habit to move about the world as if time, words, and actions were all strictly rationed. Not like the Mexicans—she would have complained.

It seemed to her that for all their passion, they were utterly inept at war. They had allowed their revolution to quagmire; by 1914 the generals and politicians had stripped it of all social and philosophic idealism. The Mexicans had a saying that Lurline liked to quote in her broken Spanish; it was a concise summary of the power struggle among the many factions:

Quítate tú para ponerme yo—which reduced all the rhetoric and the bloodshed to a simple, "Get out of my way so I can place myself."

As the mist of another winter morning burned off, the Englishwoman enjoyed her usual soft-boiled egg, toast, and black tea. Then she carried a carefully folded cloth to the flagpole that towered over her cottage. With a few deft motions, Lurline Pettigrew hoisted the Union Jack.

"God save our gracious king," she murmured softly.

She never deviated from her ritual. Every day the morning breeze would unfurl the flag and flutter it against a sky of startling clarity. In 1914 the skies of the Valley of Mexico were glass like, pierced by spiked maguey plants and soothed by snow-billowed volcanoes.

Shaggy buzzards circled St. Andrew's Park, the small British-American community of Churubusco consisting of the Country Club, pasture land, and a scattering of tile-roofed houses. *Parque San Andrés,* as it was known locally, was tied to Mexico City by Tlalpan Avenue, a wide tether of a road that connected country to city—but only physically. The little community, insular and detached, felt itself a world away from the rest of Mexico.

Lurline gazed up at a band of *zopilotes.* The vultures circled with an effortlessness that irked her, perhaps because it suggested a lazy opportunism. The whole country abounds with scavengers, she scoffed. And for a fleeting moment, she allowed herself to think of the revolution. Villa with his formidable army in the north, she easily dismissed as 'that cattle rustler.' Zapata, whose peasant soldiers controlled Xochimilco just a few miles south of her house, was a 'bother,' keeping decent men like her son-in-law from his haciendas. She declared all revolutionaries thieves, one and all. But she was even more disdainful of the counter-revolutionaries, particularly of General Victoriano Huerta, the country's latest president.

"Is the president really your grand-children's godfather?" an American neighbor had asked.

"Only to one of my grandchildren! Not to all of them!" she bristled.

Mrs. Hay was impressed nonetheless. "What is the president like?"

"Vulgar and myopic. He is no different than the rest—scoundrels all! But we need not concern ourselves, Mrs. Hay. Huerta and the revolution are a *Mexican* problem."

A more pressing problem lay snoring in her bed. Jesse. Her grandchildren called their new grandfather, *el granpa.* Lurline was forever correcting them.

"It's grand-pa! Grandpa!" she would insist.

But the children, all born and schooled in Mexico, could never quite rid themselves of the Mexican need to attach the definite article to everything, even to people. So Jesse Pettigrew was dubbed *el granpa,* and there was nothing she could do about it, any more than she could change the mood that had come over him.

When she first traded the peaceful life of widowhood for remarriage, she understood the gamble she was taking. But she had found herself irretrievably attracted to the American: to the irreverence that fueled his blue eyes; to his playful wink; to the ruddiness of his complexion when he exploded into laughter. How had he become the morose old man of late? she wondered again. He was beginning to wear her down with his moody silences and his talk of death. His death.

"What's the point to it all?" he asked rhetorically after a particularly bad morning on the golf greens. "If we're all headed for decrepitude and the grave, why not just get on with it? Why risk being taken unawares?"

"Oh, Jesse! What rot!" Lurline answered in her blunt manner, and went on pruning the roses, never imagining he meant what he said.

Pettigrew was not suicidal exactly, nor simply resigned to the inevitable. But he had grown wary in a world that seemed to blur men of noble and ignoble purpose. The coup with its assassinations had loosened the once solid ground he trod, making it slippery and treacherous; treacherous because he saw the two men he most admired—Francisco Madero and Enrique Zepeda—pit themselves against one another; slippery because he could no longer distinguish facts from propaganda.

In dreams, Pettigrew often saw himself as a boy again, walking through a stretch of dark woods on a dare, knowing full well that his older brothers were waiting to jump him. In his agony of anticipation he would deliberately call to them and give away whatever protection the dark might have given him.

However, it was Lurline who now ambushed him; pulling the bedcovers aside, she bullied him into a day with more surprises than either imagined.

"Come dear! Time to get up! It's a quarter past seven!"

"It's too damn cold!" Pettigrew muttered into his pillow as he drew up his legs.

"Come now. I'll even fetch your slippers,"—which offer led to the first fateful discovery of the day.

"What . . . what is this thing under our bed!"

He was awake now. "A coffin."

"Whose coffin?"

"Mine of course."

"Yours! Whatever do you need with a coffin?"

He pulled the blankets away from her and covered himself. "I'll have need of it soon enough."

"Over my dead body!"

One of his bushy, white eyebrows drew up quickly out of habit; she had given him the perfect chance for one of his irreverent comebacks. But he only shrugged and let the eyebrow go limp again. It was all part of the new Jesse Pettigrew. Fatalistic. Depressed. Determined to call out to death rather than be taken unaware.

"Where did it come from? I want you to send it back."

"Gayoso. And it's not going back," he answered without opening his eyes. "I like it, and that's the end of it."

He settled back. A quarter of an hour later Lurline was back, accompanied by their *mozo*, the proverbial gardener and jack-of-all-trades, and a neighbor's *mozo*. The two men dragged the coffin out; Jesse Pettigrew struggled to a sitting position. A battle erupted between husband and wife, as formidable as any clash between government troops and rebels. The hired hands disregarded the bellowing American. Following Lurline's orders, they carried the mahogany box to the carriage house in the back. She always won a shouting match by leaving the room. Victory by retreat, Pettigrew called it.

Well, that's the liveliest I've seen Jesse in a long time! she grinned.

The phone rang in the front parlor.

"Marie, dear!" Lurline greeted her daughter.

Jesse continued to rant as he dressed. When he joined his wife in the parlor, he shook a finger at her, "And I'm keeping my coffin! Nothing you . . . Lou, what's wrong!"

She held the receiver on her lap; the vacant orbs of her eyes revealed that she had just discovered that the Revolution was no longer simply a Mexican problem. Instead she answered in a strained voice, "Enrique didn't come home last night."

"Is that all?" Pettigrew breathed again. "What's new about that?"

"No. You don't understand. Enrique and his chauffeur were *waylaid* yesterday. The driver made it back late last night. He had been beaten. He said a band of men jumped them and dragged Enrique away. Marie has been up all night making frantic calls. She even rang up Huerta."

"Huerta!"

"Well he *is* the president. He has assured Marie that . . ."

"Huerta? Who the hell do you think is behind all this!" Pettigrew slumped into a chair. Despite their political differences, he recognized in the stillness of that moment how much he liked his Mexican son-in-law. Bracing an arm against his knee, he leaned forward to support his head. A moment later his fist slammed the table. "First he helps Huerta to power, Huerta the strong man who was going to turn back the clock and set things right. Then when the general plays tough he denounces him—in public no less!"

"What else could Enrique do? It's a matter of principle. Huerta continues to ignore due process of law."

"Due process . . .? This is Mexico, my dear! There's barely due process in peacetime, let alone in war! The wonder is that Enrique has lasted this long."

"Well, I am going to ring up Francis Stronge!"

He could hear her contacting the British Legation as he went out the back door. But he understood that it was all futile. "Damn it,

Enrique!" he muttered softly, his eyes moist as he thought of his vibrant son-in-law. "Damn!"

Everyone considered Enrique Zepeda's pretty wife a widow now. The ex-governor's sudden disappearance could only mean one thing: that Zepeda had joined the swelling ranks of the *desaparecidos*—the disappeared. Pettigrew needed no proof, neither the body nor a coroner's report. But Marie, his stepdaughter, lived each day mauled by hope and despair. She would leave her four children with servants and spend day after day trying to see the President. Sometimes Huerta would give her a few minutes after she had spent the entire day in the overcrowded waiting room.

He would stare at the English beauty, his friend's wife who had always seemed so aloof toward him, from the safety of his dark glasses. He would listen to her plead for news of Enrique's whereabouts. He would gaze through the thick lenses that brought her into focus only when she drew close enough for him to smell her perfume, near enough for him to see that her lovely face was becoming marked by tears and sleepless hours. Then he would smile and shake his head,

"I'm sorry, *comadre!* I have no news for you today. But of course we'll keep searching for Enrique. Meanwhile, kiss my goddaughter for me. How *is* Tiny?"

He would let himself into the shimmering lagoons that were Marie Zepeda's eyes and wait for the electric moment when she would meet his gaze. Then he would swerve to the delicate lines of her lips that moved to one dance alone: "Please help us! Tiny and her sisters keep asking for their father. Please get him back for us!"

When Marie Zepeda accepted at last that he would never help her, she stopped petitioning General Huerta. And he, needing to gaze into those green eyes of hers—whether they pleaded or condemned—began to visit her. Without warning, he would have his driver pull into the courtyard of her house, terrifying servants and children alike with his presence.

"*¡El Señor Presidente* is downstairs, *señora!*" a servant would gasp.

Marie would sit with him in the parlor upstairs, serve him Hennessey, his favorite drink any time of the day, and endure his mocking silence. A whole quarter of an hour would pass without a word being exchanged. A young Englishwoman and a Mexican general would face each other in the stiffness of a formal sitting room, listen to the ticking of the clock, and say nothing. Lurline and Jesse sat silently in the next room on one such occasion. Pettigrew puffed on a cigar and tried to read *La Semana Ilustrada.* Lurline clenched and unclenched her hands.

"This is insufferable!" she exploded at last. "Jesse, it's time you confronted the man."

El granpa groaned and kept the paper between him and his wife.

"He has no right to treat her this way! She is a British subject! You must tell him either to release Enrique, or if it is too late for that . . ." The thought drained the light from her eyes. "If it is too late for Enrique, then tell that man that he must stop harassing my daughter! Otherwise we shall take the matter up with both the British and the American governments." She wrenched the paper from his hands. "Tell him, Jesse!"

"Then you'll be asking about *my* whereabouts!"

"Nonsense! As an American citizen, you have political immunity. Besides, since you are so convinced that you are not long for this world, do something useful while you can! Go on now."

Against his better judgment, Pettigrew intercepted the General as he stepped out of the parlor and into the upper terrace. Jesse could not remember later what exactly he had said to the man in his broken Spanish, only that Huerta grabbed him roughly by the lapels and snarled,

"*¡Mire gringo desgraciado! ¡No se meta en lo que no le importa o no habrá más gringo!*"

Though he did not catch every word, Pettigrew understood the gist: don't meddle or you're dead.

Sleep was difficult from then on.

For the next few days Jesse Pettigrew stopped talking about his imminent death. There was no need to. It came looking for him late one night in the guise of Zapatista soldiers. Lurline had been the first to hear them: a faint thunder that pounded its way across the fields of St. Andrew's. She stood at a window to the left of the front door. Even before the horsemen drew up, she knew their purpose.

"Jesse! They're here for you! Quick! Run out the back door!"

Jesse was asleep. Their bedroom was the last room in the long, one-story house. She called out to him as the men dismounted. The riders, a dozen or so, wore the standard straw hat of the Zapatista soldier: wide-brimmed and sharply pointed at the crown. But these Zapatistas were wearing masks—bandanas that hid all but their eyes. One of them shouted,

"*¡Que salga el gringo¡ ¡Queremos al gringo!*"

And Lurline knew again that the revolution had never been just a Mexican problem. It stood at her door; it had devoured her daughter's husband, and now it wanted hers.

What if they go around to the back? she thought. I must let them in.

Diego Rivera. *Agrarian Leader Zapata.* Fresco, 93¾×74 in., 1931. The Museum of Modern Art, New York. Abby Aldrich Rockefeller Fund (1631.1940). ©The Museum of Modern Art/licensed by SCALA/Art Resource, New York.

"Jesse! Hurry!" she called out from her post in a voice that was half whisper, half prayer.

The riders pounded on the door. Lurline backed away and felt in the dark for a familiar box. The moment she felt the weight of the Union Jack around her shoulders, she felt the strength of a whole brigade. Drawing herself up to her full five feet eleven inches, she threw open the door and glared into luminous eyes.

"*Yo soy* English," she told them firmly. "This is my flag, *bandera.* I am a subject of King George V. *La revolución no ser para mí.*"

"*Queremos al gringo. ¡Que salga ahora mismo!*" They insisted again that the American come out.

To their astonishment, she stood on the threshold and began to sing in a robust soprano voice. "Ruuuun! They're here at the doooor-rr!"

The men hesitated, ensnared by her trills and foreign words, or perhaps by the incongruity of the serenade. Because her eyes were not wide and pleading, because she sang as if they had paid to hear her, they stood awkwardly. The leader chewed on one corner of his upper lip and stared hard at the apparition. Then he clicked his tongue.

"Está loca."

With a sweep of his arm, he pushed her aside and strode past her. His men followed, stumbling in the dark, cursing as they tripped over the hall tree overgrown with coats and umbrellas. Someone finally located a light switch. They all blinked in the sudden brightness: the large silver-haired woman with a flag draped around her like a shawl, and men with drawn machetes.

Lurline thrust out her chest, a generous one at that, and pointed to the portrait over the mantelpiece.

"Ese ser King George, mi rey, my king. You will have to answer to him."

They spilled into the rooms of her house like a muddy river overflowing its banks. Overturning small tables and lamps, they swept from room to room. She followed them to an open window in the bedroom; the curtains flapped in the night air. The men churned up her back garden, trampling the flowerbeds. When they threw back the carriage house door, she felt her knees begin to buckle.

The coffin! What if he's hiding in that damned coffin!

"Abranlo," she heard a man tell the others.

She winced as they threw open the heavy lid.

Warned by Lurline, *el granpa* had run out the back door in his nightshirt and bare feet. The winter air of the high Mexican plateau seeped into his bones. It escaped into the night in the short, frightened billows of his breath. He ran faster than he ever ran in his youth, because for all his talk about dying, dying was the last thing Jesse wanted to do that night. Terror pumped adrenaline into his body; it spurred him across pastures and into dark lanes fringed by quivering eucalyptus trees; it carried him over stones that cut his feet but could not stop him. Desperately, instinctively, he ran to the one place in all of Mexico that felt like a refuge: the country club. He panted his way to its high walls only to find the gate locked.

Pettigrew groaned; it was a low, gargled sound unlike any he had ever uttered. He stumbled and hit the ground hard. Staggering to his feet, he struggled to the water reservoir and to the gatekeeper's cottage. Bonifacio Robles opened the door a few inches.

"Qué se le ofrece?" the young man asked with a curious blend of courtesy and hostility.

"*Por Dios . . . amor . . .* For the love of God . . . *escondere, escondito . . .* Hide me!" the words spilled out, adulterated and outrageous.

All the while thunder rushed out of the dark, louder and louder. Robles recognized the old man and opened the door a little wider; his wife peered wide-eyed over his shoulder and grasped her sleeping child closer. For a few seconds no one seemed able to act. The American stared into the frightened eyes of the young couple and recognized in their dilated pupils how much he wanted to live. They in turn must have seen something of themselves in his raw fear. Bonifacio Robles nodded and grabbed the old man's arm.

He hurried Pettigrew a few hundred feet to the reservoir, St. Andrew's water supply. They came to a concrete retaining wall. "*Métase al agua, señor, y quédese alli hasta que yo le diga!*" the young man instructed.

Pettigrew climbed over the wall. The frigid water nearly cut off his breathing.

"*Por lo que más quiera, ¡no haga ruido o nos matan a todos!*"

Pettigrew did not need to be warned against making even the slightest sound. He understood the stakes for them all. Slowly, he continued to ease himself into the cold water. Every nerve shouted its alarm. Moments later he heard the riders dismounting at the gatekeeper's house. The loudness of his breathing terrified him. He concentrated on stifling it, on killing every motion of his body, every sound. He sought to merge with the wall and the water, to become part of them. Inanimate. Stillness itself.

Don't think. Don't breathe.

He heard Bonifacio Robles call out to the riders as they mounted up—something about notifying them if he saw the *gringo.* Pettigrew pressed his forehead to the wall. The men thundered off in different directions. Still he concentrated on stillness, on becoming inanimate, unthinking matter; on staying alive under that wide expanse of stars—not because their beauty awed him, but to live because he was so horrified of dying violently. And then again, perhaps their beauty did matter after all; perhaps it was enough to live without guarantees, without certainty. Perhaps he wanted to survive this night, not just because he was terrified, but because he would like to share breakfast with his wife again, and to feel the morning dew on his feet as he walked to the club, and to be able to stare across the sixth hole at those volcanoes, so utterly alien from his Missouri home, so astounding—silent giants that sneaked up on him daily, startling him again and again, as if he had no memory from the previous day.

Jesse Pettigrew shut his eyes tightly. *Oh, Lord God! Lord Jesus! Help me! Please help me!* He prayed with all the lost intensity of his childhood.

Throughout the night Huerta's hired killers terrorized the residents of St. Andrew's Park. They broke into homes and looted as they searched room after room. As the night sky faded and the *gringo* continued to elude them, they gave up on ransacking the neighborhood. They knew they had to find their man before daybreak or risk detection. They were, it turned out, local men commissioned to murder the American, locals posing as Zapatistas in order not to implicate the President who was courting American favor and could not afford American blood traced to him.

The would-be Zapatistas had their orders. In rage, in desperation, they searched the club grounds one last time.

THERE WAS AN OBITUARY OF SORTS. Enrique Zepeda's body was never returned to his family. All the newspapers carried the stories, sketchy and contradictory, of Governor Zepeda's death. Some alleged he had been shot while trying to escape the dungeons of San Juan de Ulúa; others reported that he was shot in the crossfire on the very day the Americans invaded Veracruz. The facts became the more confused when the Huerta regime collapsed a few months later. Whatever the truth, one thing was certain: that the bold, controversial, charming Enrique Zepeda had vanished like so many of his countrymen.

Jesse rarely spoke of the night he hid in St.Andrew's reservoir. His American and British neighbors respected his silence on this point. They were, however, openly curious about the bonfire Pettigrew lit behind his house.

Carefully positioned in the middle of the burning logs was a large coffin, new by the look of it and quite expensive. Jesse Pettigrew clenched a cigar between his teeth as he stoked the fire. A leprechaun-like glint had returned to his eyes.

This is a true story. Jesse and Lurline Pettigrew were the author's great great-grandparents; Enrique and Marie Zepeda were her great-grandparents. Bonifacio Robles, the young gatekeeper, is the only character whose name has been fictionalized since his actual name is not known. "The Coffin" is an excerpt from SYLVIA SHAW's recently completed nonfiction novel, *Ghosts at the Table.* The novel is the creative portion of the doctoral dissertation she defended this spring; the analytical and theoretical chapters of her dissertation examine rhetorical, historical, and narrative dimensions of the Mexican Counter-Revolution of 1913.

M. GARRETT BAUMAN

The Poem of Creation

Jirí Anderle.
Cruel Game for a Man.
Drypoint and mezzotint,
36⅛×24⅜ in., 1976.
Cincinnati Art Museum.
Gift of Anne
and Jacques Baruch.

THE WHITE KITTEN STANDS ON MY MANUSCRIPT, bats at the moving pen, then pushes his cold nose into mine. Abandoned at the local Agway, he had been under customers' feet for a week. "This is a business," the owner finally declared, "not a shelter for strays." He announced he would shoot the kitten if it was not gone by noon.

"What could I do?" my wife, Carol, said, as she handed me the dirty fur ball. "It was ten minutes to noon. The cashier was crying. Everyone applauded when I scooped the kitten up. And to think! I went in because *you* wanted a washer to stop a leaky faucet." Carol's a good salesperson. I only sighed. We take in lots of strays: hurt chipmunks, window-stunned chickadees, a watch-eyed dog, a three-legged mouse, cats who crouch for days in the back of closets, a nestling blue jay shoved from its nest, a flying squirrel and several down-on-their-luck humans. Carol says we're all essentially strays, and I can't quarrel with that.

We named this one Casper—for the ghost he almost was and for his color. Carol cured his diarrhea and bathed, wormed, groomed, fattened, vaccinated, and flea-powdered him. It's been a terrible summer for fleas, those armored jaws on springs. To kill them, you must first roll them hard between thumb and forefinger to break their legs so they can't jump. Then you crush the shell between two fingernails until there is a distinct snap. No mercy for fleas. They drive cats wild— scratching, licking, tearing in crazy circles to escape their own crawling fur. Weekly baths, dustings, even house-wide fumigation, fail.

Although we show no mercy for fleas, we ask it for our flop-eared rabbit, Crackers. One week ago while attempting to leap a fence, he fell on his jaw. It was one of those accidents you cannot explain—as unlucky as Casper was lucky. The blow drove the rabbit's jaw bone up into his middle ear, destroying his sense of balance. When he attempts to stand, he tumbles over in uncontrollable fits seeking "up." His eyes bulge, straining to hold the spinning world. He pushes against his hutch to steady himself enough to lie still, head twisted with one eye to earth, one eye to the sky. Crackers inches around his cage, feeling for gravity, trying to crawl from the vertigo.

In the past this rabbit escaped every cage we made, gnawing through two-by-fours and digging staples loose. Once, he got out just as Pow Wow, a cat who's dragged home a half-dozen wild rabbits, turned the corner. Crackers didn't hesitate. He bounded toward the cat, huge ears churning the ground like paddles. It must have been a cat's nightmare, this huge, six-legged rabbit. When Crackers treed the cat, we laughed until tears came. Pow Wow wouldn't shinny down until we caged the brute, and ever since, his world has become more uncertain.

Crackers must be hand fed grated carrot, strawberries, and raspberries, for he cannot right his head to eat. His left eye is scratched raw from rubbing the cage bottom. Gravity won't compromise to let him drink either, so I dip my finger in water so he can lick the drops with his soft, human-like tongue. Sometimes an eyedropper works. Even then, he may flip wildly two or three times if the dizziness will not give him enough tilt to swallow. The vet injected him with swelling reducer, hoping that the jaw bone might merely be pressing against the inner ear. If the bone had punctured and drained the inner ear, he'd be this way as long as he lived and there was only one humane act. This jaw-ear syndrome is common among pet rabbits bred for long ears. They're front-end heavy and more likely to land jaw first. Do the breeders think about this when they select for longer, cuter ears? Was what happened to him really an accident?

Casper, the stray white kitten, curls on my papers, so I stop writing to gaze through the window for a sign. There are always signs, for humans bring meaning to this strange world. I watch a nuthatch, hunting grubs on the maple tree upside down. He digs into crevices in the shaggy bark and plucks them out. For him upside down is right and killing is life. I wish him well. I am a killer too, and not only of fleas. I have been ruthless this week to tent caterpillars. My anger wells at those triangular webs in my fruit trees, at the leaves stripped to skeletons. I wish the birds would eat them all so I would not have to twirl a stick into the nests and rub away hundreds of lives. I wrap the nest ruins on the stick as if gathering cotton candy, scrape it onto the ground, then grind out the survivors. I am angry and sad that the universe is designed so I must kill. There are too many mouths, too much appetite in fleas, caterpillars, and humans. Murder fills every dinner plate on the planet.

Casper stretches, jumps to the floor, rubs along my leg. When I stroke his head, he crawls up my pants onto my lap and falls asleep again, perfectly secure. He does not know about death, that he was minutes away from having his head blown off. He sleeps on a man who has butchered whole tribes for each strawberry he's fed a dying rabbit. He does not know that he too will become a killer, perhaps even of rabbits. He does not know this house may burn, that terrorists may poison us, that the planet we all ride on could collide with an asteroid. No, Casper is happy. He rolls on his back, the fleas scurrying for new hideouts. One crawls over his genitals. I'll repowder him later. Let the fleas live another hour. I'm bargaining—fleas for rabbit. But I do not think life and death make deals. What is one life—rabbit, caterpillar, kitten, human—astray in the universe? Still, I stroke Casper's head to keep him purring, like a mantra for mercy.

Since Crackers has lain in his spinning cage, I have groped for a theory to account for this broken bone in my corner of the cosmos. Part of me believes it's simply the random accumulation of pain in the backwaters of the Milky Way. Meaningless, molecular rearrangements, like the staggering bag lady, the catfish in an evaporating pool, the dog living under a bridge. They happen and pass, and we invent explanations because we cannot stand not to. I suspect this may be because we live in a world that sometimes seems to defy meaning.

Yet it's also true that the atoms of the earliest trilobites and the DNA of the first Adam and Eve (whether evolving apes or clay animated by a Creator's breath) still exist. Many of these well scattered atoms walk again today in new bodies, absorbed and reshuffled. All our dust will eventually escape the grave. We are not trapped by our small notions of ourselves. I cannot believe we are condemned forever—in some hell or heaven—to our egos. What is self but a momentary arrangement of thoughts and memories, like the molecules that cohere for a time as our flesh? Souls are sunrises and rainbows whose poignant beauty and value lie in their evanescence. I prefer to think that the soul-ego leaves behind its work—its offspring, art, institutions, and history—and is then recomposed to do new work. Thoreau said in Walden, "The poem of creation is uninterrupted." He meant, I think, that our share of immortality comes from recognizing that, as part of the poem of creation, we cannot lock up our individual self, nor consider ourselves "done." Creation never ends; nor do we. The flesh we have now and our sense of self are only one line of the ever-culminating poem. Then the next line must be read.

In the Ptolemaic Universe, a concept that endured for 1,500 years, the earth was the center of the universe and all the stars arranged in logical, secure spheres by a God of hierarchy and control. Change was seen as an emanation of chaos, a threat, an evil that must be overcome. Since then, Copernicus, Newton, and Einstein have turned the universe inside out and upside down. We no longer know where we are. Chance and uncertainty principles rule; order is often only a temporary illusion we chase around our cage. Civilization has existed less than one millionth of time, if we are sure it exists yet. Life starts with the unlikeliest lucky lotto for each of us—our single sperm was the one of millions setting out that reached our mother's egg. And eerie chance may measure out our fates. I think of the woman who cried because she missed her air flight from Boston and would not get to her new grandchild that day; the businessman who snapped up her vacated seat rejoiced to have an early flight home. And then the plane was smashed into the World Trade Center. I think of the strays who find their way to my house—and of the ones we pass within inches of and never see.

Which brings me back to our rabbit who awaits the sad trip to the vet. Yes, it is only one pathetic, insignificant rabbit. But his warm, soft sides rise and fall as I stroke him. His neck stretches, and his eyes bulge wider to focus his whirling world, to find reason in the chaos. I wish my own vision was clear enough to celebrate the rendering of his cage and his leap to freedom. For now we both strain to see the vague design ahead, one eye to earth and one to sky.

M. GARRETT BAUMAN teaches at Monroe Community College in Rochester, New York. He is the author of *Ideas and Details* (Heinle and Heinle, 2001) and has written essays and fiction which have appeared in many publications.

CHUCK BERNSTEIN

A Wartime Bird Remembered

BIRD-WATCHING HAS BEEN THE FOCUS OF MY LIFE. However, throughout more than three years of active duty in three different theaters of operation during World War II, only one bird clings to memory. Perhaps that is normal, considering that I was not overseas to bird-watch and that after more than fifty years, the sounds, smells, pictures, and even some of the feelings, like aging celluloid film, have dissolved—or maybe in fact concentrated. I was on the main objective; I saw no other bird, only one, the one that probably saved my life.

AS PART OF A LARGE ASSAULT FORCE, I am leading my squad of combat infantrymen in a dawn raid on an enemy bivouac area at the base of a German forest. This woods, we are told, is dark even in daylight. So it is known to us soldiers as the "Black Forest." Though it may have been the Hurtgen or any other forest. Truthfully, when one is benumbed by war, place names don't matter much.

In total darkness compounded by dense fog, we are slowly, cautiously, silently, making our way between sky-sweeping, closely packed conifers over heavy fir and pine duff down a hill toward a meadow at the base. It is early May, and I am chilled to the bone but possibly shiver as much from trepidation. The area we are passing through, we have been cautioned, is heavily mined and booby-trapped. And an explosion, indeed the slightest noise, could bring down on us a deadly barrage of firepower from German eighty-eights and mortars, exposing us as likely to being pierced by a sharp tree splinter as by a piece of hot metal. Furthermore, stepping on a

Opposite:
Mario Merz.
Tamburino.
Enamel, acrylic, oil, spray paint, mixed media, and charcoal on canvas, 152×120×24 in., 1983–1984. Albright-Knox Art Gallery, Buffalo, New York. James S. Ely, Evelyn Rumsey Cary, and Elisabeth H. Gates Funds, 1984.

land mine or kicking a booby-trap wire would trigger a warning to the enemy, jeopardizing the entire operation, aside from leaving a GI legless or even lifeless. Dreading the consequences, I carefully try to sense where to plant each foot, sweating out with each step an explosion that could end my life.

And, if not me, who will detonate the first blast? I scan through the ghostly gloom for the members of my squad. I am, of course, concerned for the entire assault force, but worry most about my own twelve-man squad, my responsibility, *my family.* Will they—*can they*—remain silent, and will they, as instructed, maintain proper space intervals one from the other for their own protection?

We are combat-tested, but a land-mined and booby-trapped forest is new to us, and my men are young, just boys barely out of high school, over-eager to get at the foe, slap him down, and go home. Like me, they are benumbed, depressed, and weary of the horrors of war, a war so vital to our country and to the entire world. Most wear a chip like an epaulette on each shoulder, constantly daring, challenging, if not the hateful enemy, then each other.

In normal life I am no great believer in extrasensory perception, but suddenly ESP kicks in and *sensing* a wire ahead, I step to my right, then turn downhill again, where we must be getting close to our objective, for I can just make out the universally familiar soldier sounds of predawn waking in the field: the startup roar of mobile kitchen stoves, the clangor of huge pots and pans, and in guttural German, the exasperated bicker and curse of the cooks. Most telling, through the heavy stand of wet conifers comes the agonizing friendly aroma of hot coffee brewing. We should strike before we hear the clatter of metal German mess kits.

I step forward, my right foot about to descend, when suddenly from virtually underfoot there is a wild, fluttering, heart-stopping commotion. Startled, and believing I'd activated a land mind, I drop face down on the wet ground duff. And even as I drop I am aware of a flurry of activity and peripherally catch a fleeting glimpse of a tiny dark *something* flying off into the darkness.

For one awful moment I lie unmoving, and though I've not heard an explosion, I wonder if I've tripped a wire, visualizing myself like a chunk of Swiss cheese peppered with shrapnel. I listen intently waiting for perhaps a delayed concussive blast. I hear only, in rhythm with my heartbeats, the *splatsplatsplat* of accumulated mist dropping onto rock. Finding my legs intact, I mumble a prayerful thanks.

Enveloped in ghostly fog, it is only when I rise to my knees, propped up on all fours, my heart still hammering, that I begin to reconstruct what happened. Crazily, it occurs to me that at the moment of the commotion that deflected my step, I had not, as expected, seen my life flash before my eyes. What flashed before me was a bird. *It was only a bird!*

Despite catching the merest glimpse of it, I am certain only of its size. Small, perhaps the size of a European Robin. The forest gloom made it impossible to determine color or any distinguishing mark that might lead to identification, the be-all and end-all of every infantryman with active bird-watching in his past.

Then it occurs to me that this bird must have flushed from a nest. Guilt-ridden, I question whether my boot had actually hit the ground. And if so, had I crushed the nest eggs or stomped on the newborn of this tiny, frightened, defenseless avian? I had to know.

Belly down, through the thick wet carpet of forest flotsam, I snake my way back to where the bird had startled me, and feeling about, my fingers find a rough-edged cup built into the forest floor and up against and partly under what I identify as only a metal shell casing—a land mine! I recall in my peace-time back-home bird-watching life often discovering nests propped up against and even partially under dried cowflops. I had experienced birds ground-nesting in prairies and pastures, but never before in a forested minefield.

I wondered, had this avian nest builder innocently worked in a bit of trip wire leading to a detonator that if touched could send me and bird's progeny to Valhalla? At the very least my boot had been within inches of catastrophe. By flushing from its nest when it did that wee bird had probably saved my life!

I place my outstretched hand high over the nest, slowly lower it onto three warm totally intact eggs, ecstatic knowing that I'd not planted my boot on the nest or possibly the land mine. And I am astounded that with turmoil going on all around her, war or no war, this bird is *nesting*. What to the avian is merely another nesting season that will not be denied is to this GI Joe a flood of renewed hope. Life does go on.

Through the darkness and clinging fog, I peer in vain to find the fragile feathered female that panicked and fled, perhaps saving my life, and indeed, the entire assault, but it is hopeless. And I cannot linger.

SHAKEN AND AGHAST both at what my booted foot had almost undone at the nest and the frightening reality of how close I had come to blowing myself to bits, I move on down the hillside, angrier and more cynical than ever, my rifle at the ready, sobbing inwardly for the avian race, silently cursing yet sorrowing for the human race, and wondering whether that frantic frightened little bird and I would survive to another nesting time.

CHUCK BERNSTEIN spent three-and-half years in the infantry in the European and Pacific theaters in World War II. He has been an author and editor of birding columns in *Birdwatcher's Digest* and *Birding* magazine and is author of *The Joy of Birding* (Cavez Press, 1947).

PART II

Self-Discovery

looking east
each morning through the trees,
the river—
each morning through the trees,
a different river
—ART STEIN

As we go into depth in ourselves, oddly enough,
we run into a wisdom greater than our own.
This is the omniscient One. In its vicinity, wisdom
spontaneously arises. This means that, as simple
humans, we have ourselves backward. We take
the body and senses as real, but the outer us is really our
least aspect. Deep within, feeling, love,
and wisdom are our real selves. Being within, in
touch with these greater aspects, is to be
in the vicinity of the One.
—WILSON VAN DUSEN
The Design of Existence

WILSON VAN DUSEN

The Gift of Tears

An Ancient Tradition

Adolph Gottlieb.
The Seer.
Oil on canvas,
59¾×71⅝ in., 1950.
The Phillips Collection,
Washington, D.C.
Acquired 1952.

MANY YEARS AGO—after a long time of being busy with other things—I returned to the direct experience of God. As the mystical union blossomed again (I had first known it in childhood), I became concerned to know within the experience what was mine and what was God's. I asked God for some sign so I could tell the difference.

Shortly afterwards I was speaking on spiritual matters to a class of college students. The Gift of Tears turned up! I tried desperately to conceal it, but it broke through every concealment, for—in response to my request—tears now marked what was God's. . . . Soon my handkerchief was a soggy mess, and a kind student supplied me with a box of tissues that I shortly ran through. How paradoxical! Here I was merely trying to present the spiritual in a form understandable to the students, and the spiritual itself was interfering. Seeing myself now as impaired, I quit all public speaking for some years. Eventually, however, I got the idea to explain to my audience this strange gift early in my presentations. By revealing rather than concealing, perhaps I could get by better. It seemed to work. There were fewer tears, and I could make a halfway-decent presentation.

Meanwhile I turned to colleagues in psychology for help. They had not a clue. Then one day, in the literature of the Eastern Orthodox Church, I found a direct, clear mention of the gift of tears: a monk searching for a teacher would be best off going to one who had the gift of tears because that teacher *feels* the truth and thus has a deeper understanding of it. Here was a major clue—an ancient tradition behind my tears: the whole concept of *felt understanding* came to the fore. An example might be if a significant loved one has just died. You prepare a little talk on your loved one to be given at the funeral. In your own mind, you say it well. But, as you speak at the funeral, you begin to notice strong feelings coming to the surface. You try your best to cover these up, but tears burst forth and interfere with your speech. Your feelings do not respect time, place, reputation, or any external concerns. You had a mountain of emotions associated with the departed. They are part of the very truth you were trying to calmly present. This situation is exactly analogous to the gift of tears, only the beloved is the spiritual itself. Feeling is actually a deeper understanding.

THERE ARE OTHER DIMENSIONS TO THIS EXPERIENCE: as though deeper understanding of the spiritual in general is not the issue but rather some specific aspect of the spiritual. For me, whenever I touch on the universal that binds us into a unity, tears are awakened. Tears may be evoked, for instance, when I am lecturing on the International Navigation Rules, the rules for the conduct of vessels in sight of each other. Why? Because this subject is near that very universal that binds us into one. This aspect of the spiritual may also account for my tears becoming more prevalent when with an audience, for in public speaking I feel bound together with my listeners; the situation itself thus elicits the complex. But in addition something transcendent is emerging that I clearly do not understand well.

In my last talk I wrote into my outline that I should explain the gift of tears in the beginning of the speech. But suddenly, even before the explanation, I came into a full-body convulsion of feeling. I was simply overwhelmed, with eyes closed, both hands tightly clasped, not breathing. Long ago someone asked what the direct experience of God was like, and I answered that it was like being run over by a locomotive with a sense of the overwhelming power of God. But, in the speech I was giving, the locomotive came before my explanation. It lasted only a few moments, but it took time to start breathing again and to get a semblance of control.

Inwardly it is like experiencing the full intensity of meaning all at once, which is hopeless to try to explain to my listeners, especially to the coldly rational. Some in the audience feel I must be on drugs or mentally unbalanced; in fact, a counter-culture young man once complimented me on taking dope before my talk. Some in the audience empathize with me. Some have said their own tears now make better sense to them. Knowing my tendencies, I brought three handkerchiefs to this talk and pretty well finished all three. Yet I also felt unusually clear on spiritual matters and was surprised at some of the wisdom shown in my own answers in the questions-and-comment period. Note I do not take credit for this wisdom. For a long while I have felt like an old violin, at times played by expert hands, and, of course, each experience of the Divine brings in more wisdom. Each burst of feeling in the gift of tears is more of the Divine, enlightening the foolish and limited self.

In my work with people who are on the verge of the experience of God, their unbidden tears are an excellent sign of their intuition of the spiritual. It means these individuals are often in the presence of a wisdom greater than their own. They may not understand through the intellect, but they can begin to understand through their feelings. Usually these people are wise enough to suspect that their depth of feeling indicates the wisdom being given is from beyond their own limited powers. So those with this gift should honor it by trying to remain in the feeling and by searching within it for what is being given. There may not be a specific content or message. It may be that the person is simply being shown the real life of which our daily life is but a limited ray or aspect.

THAT SUGGESTION OF A TRADITION BEHIND THE GIFT OF TEARS led me to a wider search, though I never found a sign of it in religions other than the Christian. I nevertheless assume knowledge of the gift probably exists in all religions. It is hard to find, however, even in Christianity; indeed, most of Christianity seems to have rushed on to newer things. But, even today, the Eastern Orthodox Church remains in a mystical tradition quite like the Christianity of its early fathers. *The Philokalia* is a collection of their writings up to the fifteenth century—a four-volume treasury, recording experiences of certain Saints who had full religious lives.[1] There are some one hundred references to tears in these volumes. For example:

> *. . . then the tears of joy and understanding will well up copiously within you and you will drink from their plenitude.*
>
> —ST. PETER OF DAMASKOS, VOL. III, P. 99

Do not grow conceited if you shed tears when you pray. For it is Christ who has touched your eyes and given you spiritual sight.

—ST. MARK THE ASCETIC, VOL. I, P. 111

First pray for the gifts of tears so that through sorrowing you may tame what is savage in your soul. And having confessed your transgressions to the Lord, you will obtain forgiveness from Him. Pray with tears and all you ask will be heard. For the Lord rejoices greatly when you pray with tears. If you do shed tears during your prayer, do not exalt yourself, thinking you are better than others. For your prayer has received help so that you can confess your sins readily and make your peace with the Lord through your tears. Therefore do not turn the remedy for passions into a passion, and so again provoke to anger Him who has given you this grace.

—EVAGRIOS THE SOLITARY, VOL. I, P. 58

. . . how impossible it is to conform to God without complete stillness; how stillness gives birth to ascetic effort, ascetic effort to tears, tears to awe, awe to humility, humility to foresight, foresight to love; and how love restores the soul to health and makes it dispassionate, so that one then knows that one is not far from God.

—ABBA PHILIMON, VOL. II, P. 345

These people knew something of spiritual tears. How comforting it was for me to feel a part of this ancient tradition. But, why hasn't anything on tears turned up in other major religions? Surely a concordance on the *Koran* would show it; I cannot believe it would exist only in Christianity. God is omnipresent, everywhere. The Holy Spirit is the resident Divine, there to accompany and aid the individual.

OTHER GIFTS are sometimes given as a mode of personal communication between the believer and God. The mystic Emanuel Swedenborg received a flaming light that dazzled his outer physical eyes as well as his inner spiritual eyes.[2] He came to see the flame as illustrating a difference between lesser spirits and the love and warmth of the celestial. It turned up when God wished to convey to him a deeper celestial meaning to what he was studying. The heat of the flame represented divine love, and its light symbolized divine wisdom. The combination of love and wisdom is a central aspect of all he was shown. The flame was then God's way of saying, "There is a deeper aspect here."

In Swedenborg's exploration of heaven and hell he came to describe another heavenly phenomenon. Heaven, he found, is divided into the spiritual level versus the celestial or heavenly.

> The angels in God's heavenly kingdom far surpass the angels of the spiritual kingdom in regard to wisdom and splendor because they accept God's divine nature on a deeper level. They live in love for him, and are therefore more intimately united to him. The reason for their excellence is that they have accepted divine truths directly into their lives and continue to do so, rather than taking them into memory and thought first, the way spiritual angels do. This means they have them engraved on their hearts and grasp them, virtually see them, within themselves. They never calculate whether or not they are true.[3]

The gift of tears is the breakthrough to this heavenly realm, and this is the inner nature of the gift of tears. One suddenly runs into what is engraved on the heart, and the feeling around it is released. It is felt meaning, full of life. This is a different level of understanding than that from the spiritual level of heaven. There one can coolly examine whether a thing is true or not. At the celestial level one is suddenly in the presence of truth that is full of feeling because it is one's very life.

> People like this know instantly, from an inflow from God, whether the truth they are hearing is actually true. The Divine flows directly into our intentions, and indirectly, through our intentions into our thinking.[4]

> I have been granted knowledge of this through an abundance of experience. I have heard angels discover a person's life simply by listening. They have told me that they know everything about another person's life from a few individual ideas because these enable them to know the person's ruling love, which contains everything in a pattern. This is all that our "book of life" is.[5]

> Since angels' language corresponds to the affections of their love, . . . we can see how elegant and delightful their conversation is. It affects not only the ears but also the deeper levels of the minds of those who hear it. There was one particular hard-hearted spirit with whom an angel talked, and eventually he was so moved by what the angel was saying that he burst into tears, saying that he couldn't help it, love was talking, and he had never cried before.[6]

The gift of tears may happen during breakthroughs to this higher level of experiencing. It simply appears; it breaks through to the celestial, and is quite beyond individual control—as indicated by my various efforts to control or conceal it. I know a minister with a parallel experience. He finds that the gift of tears aids his work as a minister, that women seem to more readily empathize with it, while men tend to be more skeptical. Whereas I find that the gift of tears interferes in my making an educational talk, the gift serves him well.

There are, in fact, a host of possible personal forms of communication between the individual and the Divine. I know of two other forms that showed up in other mystics. One curiously is an actual sound in the world at the very instant this person thinks of God. Others hear the same sound in the world, but it means nothing to them because they cannot see that it is timed to one's thought of God. Other gifts of the Holy Spirit described in Isaiah 11.2 and Galatians 5:22–23 include the great gifts of wisdom, understanding, fortitude, piety, and fear of God. But these have been little noticed. Were my gift of tears not seen by others and inquired about, I too would not have spoken of it. Why? Because it seems immodest and easily criticized. And the spiritual person would rather be silent than open up spiritual matters to unseemly debate. This is probably the very reason this ancient area of human experience is so little known. But if you experience tears in spiritual matters, honor them and look at what you are being shown, for when the mind is stilled, you can feel the invisible within the visible.

> *A heart that has been completely emptied of mental images gives birth to divine, mysterious intellections that sport within it like a fish and dolphins in a calm sea. The sea is fanned by a soft wind, the heart's depth by the Holy Spirit.*
>
> —ST. HESYCHIOS THE PRIEST, PHILOKALIA, VOL. I, P. 190

Notes

1. Saint Nikodimos of the Holy Mountain, et al. *The Philokalia.* 4 v. Faber & Faber, London, 1979 to 1995.
2. Emanuel Swedenborg. *The Spiritual Diary.* 4 v. The Academy, Bryn Athyn (Pennsylvania), 1994. Paragraphs 3629 and 3630. In Swedenborgian studies it is customary to cite Swedenborg's paragraph numbers rather than pages, since they are uniform in all editions.
3. Emanuel Swedenborg. *Heaven and Hell.* New Century translation. Swedenborg Foundation, West Chester (Pennsylvania), 2000. Paragraph 25.
4. Op.cit. Paragraph 26.
5. Op.cit. Paragraph 236.
6. Op.cit. Paragraph 238.

WILSON VAN DUSEN is a clinical psychologist and author of numerous books on the inner world.

ANN JAUREGUI

Three Tales from Serendip

Bird-form finial. Colombia: Zenú, gold, $3^{13}/_{16} \times 2^{9}/_{16} \times 4^{1}/_{4}$ in., c. 500–1500 AD. Dallas Museum of Art. The Nora and John Wise Collection. Gift of Mr. and Mrs. Jake L. Hamon, the Eugene Mc Dermott Family, Mr. and Mrs. Algur H. Meadows, and the Meadows Foundation, and Mr. and Mrs. John D. Murchison (1976.W.438).

I

A strange bird, with golden wings and eyes like fire, dipped down out of the sky. It was seen, however, by only a handful of children. King Jaiya missed it, for he had many burdens which made his head bend low with anxiety.

—*THE THREE PRINCES OF SERENDIP*, ELIZABETH JAMISON HODGES

ONCE UPON A TIME, in a land far away, there lived three young princes. So begins an ancient tale, told through time in many tongues, about the three young princes of Serendip who are sent out from their island kingdom of emerald mountains, now called Sri Lanka, to the great beyonds of the world in search of character, compassion, and wisdom. And something else, too.

As the story goes, King Jaiya summons his three sons, Balakrama, Vijayo, and Rajahsingha. They must journey, he tells them, in search of a secret formula called *Death to Dragons.* This is the magic fluid which will rid the waters of the dangerous monsters who have plagued the otherwise serene kingdom of Serendip for so long.

A magnificent bird appears throughout the tale, a golden bird with eyes like fire. Only the traveling princes and a handful of children see this great bird when it dips down out of the sky. They look up and exclaim with joy at the marvelous sight. But many others — people who are asleep or preoccupied with trouble, people whose heads are bent low with anxiety—cannot see it.

In the end it is this great bird who will convey the magic fluid in a silver cylinder in his beak, extinguish the dragons forever, and restore serenity to the grateful citizens of Serendip. And what does the mysterious fluid turn out to be? Why nothing more or less, we learn, than the tears the princes shed upon coming into a valley whose crops and villages had been destroyed by fire, tears collected by the magic bird.

And so the author, Horace Walpole, first English teller of this tale, coins the happy word "serendipity." Sometimes serendipity is used to mean a lucky or providential accident or coming together of seemingly unrelated events. But Walpole tells us it is the princes themselves who are *possessed* of serendipity. "As their highnesses traveled," he writes in 1754, "they were always making discoveries of things they were not in quest of"—including their final discovery that tears of compassion slay dragons. Today, true to Walpole, the *Random House Dictionary* defines serendipity as "the faculty for making desirable discoveries by accident."

In this fairy tale we encounter a purposeful and continuous universe. The surprising and marvelous is ever-present, and the three princes are endowed with the natural capacity to apprehend it. Serendipity will sustain and guide them in all their journeys. All they must do is look up.

II

ONE DAY A PSYCHOTHERAPY CLIENT OF MINE came in for her regular appointment looking uncharacteristically fitful and pale. Trouble hung around her like a shroud. What had happened?

She gathered herself and told me that it was her birthday and that she had not heard anything from her family. She had always felt closest to her mother, who had died several years earlier. After her mother's death, the others in the family had converted from wayward Catholicism to a fundamentalist Christian faith, and they had not been in touch with her for more than a year.

"We don't understand each other at all anymore," she said in a tight voice, too hardened around the pain to cry. "They think I'm damned, and there's no way they can reach me. There's no way I can reach them. I've lost my mother, and now I've lost all of them. It's making me sick."

Her suffering filled the room.

On an impulse I asked her if she knew the work of physician and author Larry Dossey. I told her something about his interest in recent prayer studies which seem to show that prayer—especially "non-directed" prayer, like "Thy will be done"—has a positive effect on distant people, whether they are aware that they are being prayed for or not. It also seems to have a positive effect on those who are doing the praying.

"What is your prayer life like?" I asked her.

She was surprised and a little hesitant. "Nobody's ever asked me before."

"Maybe if we lived in a less secular culture we would ask each other more often," I said. "Maybe we would meet in the road and ask, 'How's your love life going? How's your prayer life going?'"

"I never talk about it to anybody," she said. "I guess not even to myself. When I was afraid I might miscarry, I said that prayer in *Frannie and Zooey*."

"Remind me."

"Oh, you know, 'Have mercy on me' over and over."

"How did you pray in your Catholic school days?"

"I said the rosary a lot. When my father had his heart attack, I would say the rosary all night on my knees." She paused. "My knees . . . I developed something, I think it was called cellulitis. The doctor said, 'Have you been scrubbing a lot of floors?'"

"What did you tell him?"

"Yes. I said yes. My mother told me I'd better stop praying all night.'"

"And so you did?"

"And so I did," she said. "I'm not sure I ever really prayed again."

"If you were to pray about you and your family now, in some 'Thy will be done' way. . . ."

The room fell silent. Then she said, almost too quietly to be heard, "Something is happening to me."

Something was happening to me, too.

Her hands lay open on her lap now, soft, and tears were streaming down her cheeks.

"Something wonderful has come into the room," she said. She looked around as if to see it in the air and laughed a sparkling laugh that sounded like singing. She fluttered her hands and shook her head as if to protest this laughing. "What's happening here? This just came, didn't it!"

"You know," she said after a while, "my husband has printed a collection of about fifteen of my short stories. I wasn't going to give copies to my family, but now I am. Now I am. I see myself throwing paper airplanes over the wall. It doesn't matter what happens to them."

III

ONE SUNDAY MORNING, driving across town on quiet streets, something fluttering caught the corner of my eye. About a block away, tiny flags were waving on clotheslines in the middle of the street. It was a couple of weeks after the events of September 11, 2001, and there had been anthrax. I was still dazed. Everybody was. But I remembered hearing about a neighborhood candlelight vigil that had grown into a nightly event and an impromptu shrine. I pulled over.

Right in the middle of a three-corner intersection was a roped-off triangle. From potted plants brought out from neighbors' houses, clotheslines had been strung, and from them flew hundreds of handwritten wishes, many from children, like little flags. On the pavement inside the triangle was a sudden lawn of Astroturf with real and artificial flowers, candles and puddles of melted wax, a vigil invitation on an easel, stuffed animals a little worse for the weather, and a globe of the world.

I was contemplating this apparition when a woman came walking up from another direction. She slowed her step, brushed back smartly cut hair, and stared. She and her son had seen the wish cards as they were driving by, she said after a while. He had gone on to get gas, but she had jumped out.

"What is this?" she whispered, as if we were in church.

We began to work our way along the lines of notes.

Some of the wishes were prayers for victims of the September attacks and condolences for their families. A child offered thanks for rainbows, and waterfalls, and a cat named Jack. Another had written in painstakingly careful letters, "To every little child who is afraid, I hope you are feeling better."

We read all the way around, and then all the way around again.

"My son is a freshman here at the university," she said finally, introducing herself. "I've been in town for Parents' Weekend."

"There were events on campus?" I asked her. We were still whispering. The notes fluttered silently.

"Panel discussions these past two days," she said. "Professors from all departments trying to make sense of 9/11. Engineers talking about the construction of the buildings, public-policy people, political scientists, religious scholars, talking about the basic tenets of Islam—it's been wonderful. I've wanted to be a student again. But this," she said, indicating the improbable triangle park with a motion of her hand, "this . . ."

A neighbor came out, rolling her garbage can along, and began to clear away melted candles and faded flowers.

"We had no idea when we began," the neighbor said, realizing we were looking to her for the story of how the shrine had come to be. "We've collected 1,700 wish cards written by friends and visitors from all over the country and from other countries too. There has been healing for us in the sharing."

A tall young man drove up now and got out. He looked strikingly like his mother.

"What's going on?" he asked. Then, in a whisper, "What's going on?"

His mother nodded at the cards and waited as he read a few.

"We've never been a church-going family," she began, "and I haven't thought very much about prayer. . . ."

Her son was watching her closely, worried about her tears.

"This makes no sense, and I don't expect anyone back home to understand it." She slipped her arm through his. "But this is the most joyful day of my life."

Once upon a time . . .

Standing at the entrance of his rustic house, the farmer raised his eyes to watch a wild hare as it leapt up the steep sides of a mountain. Then abruptly he noticed a strange bird. It had golden wings and eyes like fiery stars.

Note

Hodges, Elizabeth J. *The Three Princes of Serendip.* 1964. New York: Atheneum. A children's book based upon an ancient tale as retold by Horace Walpole.

ANN JAUREGUI is a practicing psychotherapist in Berkeley, California, and adjunct professor at the Graduate School of Professional Psychology, John F. Kennedy University. She is the author of *Epiphanies: A Psychotherapist's Tales of Spontaneous Emotional Healing* (Prima Publishing), to be published in Spring 2003.

ELLEN DUDLEY

Pacific

At fifteen hundred feet and nine miles in
we can smell the ocean today.
And out there it's blue glass, pacific,
kind—as if you'd bob in place
and the currents out past the point
wouldn't take you to the nearest
and next continent: Antarctica.
Huge and blue and smelling not
of death and brine as the Atlantic does,
but of enormity and of the whale breaching
off the point last night, immune
to currents—breeding, in the frigid waters
off Alaska, feeding here.
She makes us draw our breath—or lose it.
And miles out there, an island forms
boils three thousand feet down:
Loihi, named before its birth by
a species that may well kill itself
before the new land bursts, heaves,
makes its way to air. Ten thousand
years we give this island we have named
before it lurches from the sea, graceful
and enormous and unaccountable
for what we call it: land, whale,
volcano . . . our earth.

ELLEN DUDLEY is the author of *Slow Burn* (Provincetown Arts Press, 1997). Her work has appeared or is forthcoming in *TriQuarterly, Agni, Massachusetts Review, The Poetry Miscellany, Phoebe,* and other magazines. She is the winner of a Vermont Council on the Arts Fellowship and is founding editor–publisher of the *Marlboro Review.* She lives in Marlboro, Vermont, where she is co-owner of a construction company.

ANITA SWANSON

Surprised by Grief

Richard M. Ferris. *Chamber Organ.* Wood and various other materials, 104×58 in., ca. 1850. The Metropolitan Museum of Art, New York. Gift of Hans H. Schambach, 1986.

I LAST SAW HIM as he lay dying in the hospital though I had not gone willingly to his bedside. When the doctor called early that morning to say they needed a Do Not Resuscitate order, I told him to call someone else. The doctor responded, "He told us he wanted you."

He'd been diagnosed with pancreatic cancer and, by the time I arrived, obstructive jaundice had turned his body an intense lime-green. Surrounded by the bleached whiteness of the hospital sheets, his face and arms appeared to give off an almost incandescent glow. It was heart wrenching to bear witness to his body, once so filled with life now diseased and dying.

When he spoke, he spoke only of regret and wanting another chance at life. "I'd do so many things differently," he said in a voice so weak I had to strain to hear it. "So many things." I reached for his hand and was shocked to see he still wore his wedding band. I'd taken mine off years ago.

Get-well cards were stacked high upon his bedside table, many from concerned members of his church, others from people high in theological circles. When I remarked on the abundance of well wishers, he barely nodded his head in response. As an award-winning conductor and soloist, he'd wanted fame from the world through his music, and God had given him fame through his music from the church. It was a gift he never wanted. A blessing he was never able to receive.

Overwhelmed by sadness, I sat at his bedside and wept. Two days later, while our daughters were in school, he died.

Over a thousand people attended his funeral, but I sat alone in my grief, and the depth of my pain surprised me.

If someone had told me I'd suffer such profound sorrow at his passing, I would not have believed it. I didn't think people grieved over ex-husbands. And even if they did, I certainly would not grieve over mine. There'd been too many years filled with anger and pain, and too few years filled with forgiveness and love.

But in the weeks and months following his funeral, I came to a realization that brought a new understanding to my sorrow. I realized I'd forgotten how much I used to love this man. I'd forgotten, you see, because our love had happened years earlier—another time, another place—another life. I also came to understand that my grief was not for the love that had died so many years ago. My pain was for a lifetime of worn-out hopes. My sadness was for all our dreams that had burned with such white-hot intensity when we were young, and that flickered in my heart. Still. What would become of all our dreams now, now that death had taken the final embers away?

I was surprised by my grief when my ex-husband died. I was healed through the process of mourning. Acceptance did not come easily. I fought what my heart already knew. That in death he had become what he'd always been: the man I'd once chosen to marry and the father of my children.

I see him in their faces. I feel him in their laughter. And, when I hear them singing, I know his voice has flown from heaven's corridors to remind me that he has become a part of me—forever.

Born and raised in Minneapolis, ANITA SWANSON graduated from Northwestern Hospital School of Nursing before marrying and moving to Los Angeles, where eventually she enjoyed success in the theater community in numerous plays. She has appeared in national television commercials, was featured in a children's show, and was part of the prestigious West Coast Ensemble Theatre Company. She is a member of the Screen Actors Guild.

MICHAEL NETHERCOTT

Adventures in Archaeology

NINA'S WEEKEND HAD GONE FABULOUSLY ASTRAY. From her Friday night dinner party (flaccid soufflé and sloppy-drunk neighbors) through Saturday's day trip (traitorous road maps and college-frazzled daughter) right on into that evening's crescendo (volcanic phone debate with ex, followed by Big Festival of Insomnia.) With this morning's three-hour dragnet for her renegade collie, you couldn't ask for a snappier couple of days.

Now, on this Sunday beach, Nina resigned herself to a low chair and watched blankly as happy families jostled the lake waters. Soon, mercifully, the curtain would drop on this Hamlet of a weekend. She burrowed her toes into hot sand, discovering at once a pleasing coolness. Perhaps she could drill deeper and deeper to fully plant herself in some numbing ostrich limbo. Truth be told, many of her recent weekends had failed her. And, yes, the weekdays, as well.

Her left big toe struck something. Nina reached down and yanked free a small plastic-coated card encrusted with dirt. She wiped it clean and stopped breathing for several seconds. Here was her own face, miniaturized, younger and a bit leaner, gazing up at her cheerfully and unfathomably. It took a full minute for the reality to sink in: this was an old driver's license of hers. Yes, she remembered now—she had lost one once, but that was ten years ago, no, more like fifteen. The date on the license bore this out. Right. She had lost it here by the lake.

She studied the returned face for a long time. The smile, a grin really, especially captivated her. Though entombed lo these many years, it had not lost its easy gleam. The smile and the face and the miniature woman still possessed the knack for happiness. Nina fought back an impulse to draw the image to her lips and kiss it. She was, after all, on public property.

A Frisbee whooshed past her, stroking her hair. Its master, an earnest little boy, ran up brandishing apologies. Nina laughed.

MICHAEL NETHERCOTT's short stories, poems and scripts have appeared in various national periodicals including *Fantasy and Science Fiction, Cobblestone, Hopscotch,* and *Plays, the Drama Magazine for Young People.*

DAVID L. BERGMANN

The Beekeeper

PUTNAM FLINT WILL BE THE FIRST TO ADMIT that he was never much of a student. By the time he reached America's oldest preparatory school, the Governor Dummer Academy in South Byfield, Massachusetts, he already was a veteran of several schools, including Milton Academy's lower school, Derby Academy, and two Boston-area public schools. The headmaster's letters to Flint's parents consistently expressed concern over Flint's academic work, but also an obvious admiration for the boy who seemed to be involved in every activity on campus. Flint explains today, "I wanted my place in the sun at school; I knew I was no scholar—that's why I was into so many extracurricular activities."

But the boy's middling grades weren't the result of mediocre intellect or insufficient application; they arose from an affliction that hadn't even been identified in Putnam's school days, the 1930s: dyslexia. Flint himself wouldn't discover until forty-three years later that he suffers from this language-processing handicap: printed material looks jumbled, making reading extremely difficult and mathematics nearly impossible. Despite his impairment, Flint compensated with ability and talents in other areas. His manual dexterity, which he used to "repair watches for pin money," has always been excellent, Flint says, self-effacingly showing off a recently blackened fingernail—the victim of his constant tinkering.

Opposite: Putnam Flint, Photographer. *George W. Adams.* 1935.

Teachers elsewhere had lost patience with young Flint, but—despite his dyslexia—not Governor Dummer's masters. "The impact of MacMurphy, Tom Mercer, Art Sager, Ben Stone, Buster Navins, and Bill Jacob . . ." Flint says, tapping his desktop repeatedly for emphasis as he names the 'Old Guard' teachers, "put a stamp on me that said, 'Putty, you're okay.' The masters preserved my spirit and let me know they thought I was a worthwhile human being."

Dottie, Flint's wife, said, "They allowed him a freedom that he'd never had before. They allowed him to work at his own pace."

Among Flint's greatest influences was George W. Adams, who, although not a faculty member, was an alumnus (class of 1873) and campus fixture. Adams lived near the academy. He sometimes gave the impression of being something of a hick but in actuality was a classicist, ". . . a naturalist, antiquarian, craftsman, and philosopher," according to the 1935 yearbook. He also "kept the Academy bees," an avocation that captured Flint's interest—to the exclusion of other scholastic activities, including Mr. Jacob's Latin class. Flint says he always would take a window seat in Mr. Jacob's classroom "because Mr. Adams would come and do his bees at that time every day," and Flint could watch. "Mr. Jacob knew this and was very kind to tutor me in Latin at his home later." The experience left Flint with a greater admiration for the Governor Dummer faculty, and he was "stung with the love of beekeeping, which has always stayed with me." Flint fails to mention, however, that he is deathly allergic to bee stings and must carry a syringe of adrenaline to counter their effects.

Flint graduated from the academy in 1937, winning "several prizes on the commencement platform," as the headmaster wrote Flint's parents. He spent the next year "taking college boards again and again" at The New Preparatory School in Harvard Square and going to the Harvard summer school.

"I was then admitted to Bowdoin underneath the threshold of the door," Flint says, "which later opened wider in the opposite direction." By more or less mutual decision, Flint left Bowdoin after one semester. "The Bowdoin experience was a horror," he says, filled as it was with "essay assignments and reading." He jokes now that he got As in two subjects: public speaking and what he refers to as "the social aspect" of college life. A former member of his academy's glee club, Flint became a founding member of the college's famed "Meddiebempters" in his short time at Bowdoin.

While Flint worked as a scientific glassware inspector for a few years, war was breaking out in Europe and Japan. He tried to enlist in the Navy, but the Army draft got to him first, placing him in the infantry. Flint rose quickly through the enlisted ranks and soon was shipped off to Ft. Hood, Texas, for Officer's Candidate School. It was during that experience that Flint met his bride-to-be, and they were married in February, 1944. Seven months later, he was shipped off to command a platoon of tank destroyers in France and Germany—an assignment he blames today for his hearing impairment. It was during that tour of duty that the first of the Flints' four children was born.

The Beehive.
Silk embroidery
and watercolor on silk,
1800–1820.
Abby Aldrich Rockefeller
Folk Art Museum,
Colonial Williamsburg
Foundation,
Williamsburg, Virginia.

Returning to the States, Flint went to work for a cousin as a manufacturer's agent, selling "particle-reduction machinery." He was selling this grinding machinery from the trunk of his car, one day showing a Vermont maple sugar manufacturer how his equipment could grind up the manufacturer's product, then driving a short distance to demonstrate the same process at a talc quarry—using the same machine.

After ten years with the company, Flint—again, with no formal engineering background—developed a batter mixer, and soon thereafter bought the company he'd been working for and renamed it.

Anyone who has ever eaten prepared foods probably has benefited from Flint's work. Companies like Campbell Soup, Gorton's, Heinz, Con-Agra, Howard Johnson, Mrs. Paul's, Tyson, Swanson, and Van De Kamp's use Flint's small but highly profitable Wilevco. Specifically, they share a machine that Flint developed and has manufactured to the present: the first automatic batter mixer with viscosity control. In laymen's terms, Flint created a machine that will turn out food-coating batters and keep them at precise thicknesses and temperatures. According to Flint's clients, who fairly burst with praise for Wilevco, this seemingly simple (but actually complex) invention has saved millions of dollars and assured quality control never before achieved. It surprises no one meeting him today that Flint is a successful inventor; the great surprise comes when one learns that he has neither a formal engineering background *nor* a college degree.

Over lunch in a Thai restaurant, Flint reflects a moment on a fiery morsel of Thai food and says his dyslexia may have been a blessing. "I was never taught the traditional approach to problems," he says, explaining that he, therefore, never has been constrained by conventional thinking.

This unconventional thinking brought to mind an experience Flint had about seventy years ago. He had become very fond of Mr. Adams, sort of a grandfather he never had. One weekend he pedaled over from school to Mr. Adams' house arriving as he was "doing his bees." Mr. Adams said,

> Let me tell you a story, Put: One day a student came up from the Massachusetts Institute of Technology down in Cambridge. The student asked me, "How many times do a bee's wings flutter in a second?" I told him I didn't know but give me a few minutes. I went to the kitchen, got an empty mayonnaise jar, punched some holes with an ice pick in the metal cover, and returned to the beehive. I carefully took a handful of bees, eased them into the jar, and put the cover on. "Now, Sonny," I said, "follow me." We went into the house where I opened the cover on the piano and shook the jar. The bees made a clear buzz that I picked out as the note two octaves above middle C. "Look up the frequency for that note, Sonny," I said, "and you will have your answer!"

"*Quod erat demonstrandum!*" Flint exclaimed with his impish smile.

DAVID L. BERGMANN is a writer based in Massachusetts.

FREDRICK ZYDEK

Dreams That Fade before Morning

Each of these dreams is on an inward journey.
They go deeper than the mind's eye can see,
seldom stray close enough to the surface
to slip into what the memory makes of such things.

These are dreams that blink out before dawn.
Sometimes I can recall a slight phantom outline
of the plot. More often than not, nothing.
Even their fragrance flickers and is gone.

I must descend into these dreams without paper
or pen. I may wake with some hint that I've
visited them, but they become so much like ether
there is no vocabulary that can name their parts.

Some mornings I'm sure I spent the night dreamless.
Usually by the time I'm into my second cup of coffee,
the memory nudges up against the host of a dream.
I know better than to call its name or wonder

how we spent the night. I've learned to trust
these things, to let them go about their business
unhampered by a curiosity that doesn't seem to know
that some memories were meant to set like the sun.

FREDRICK ZYDEK is the author of five collections of poetry. His work has appeared in *The Antioch Review, The Hollins Critic, Michigan Quarterly Review, Poetry, Poetry Northwest,* and other journals. *T'Kopechuck: The Buckley Poems* is forthcoming from Winthrop Press later this year. Formerly a professor of creative writing and theology at the University of Nebraska and later at the College of Saint Mary, he is now a gentleman farmer when not writing. Most recently he has accepted a post as editor for *Lone Willow Press.*

JAMES O. LOGAN

How Did Johnny Die?

THE THIRTIETH INFANTRY DIVISION wiggled down the cargo nets hung on the sides of British Navy boats, landing on the Normandy Peninsula, Omaha Beach, 10 June 1944. But this day, there was no enemy. The first Allied invaders had cleared the beaches, killed hundreds of Germans, and destroyed the largest concrete and steel fortifications ever seen by those who wore the shoulder patch of Andrew Jackson, "Old Hickory."

Once ashore and treading on French land for the first time, we climbed the hastily-built road. Following orders to change our wet socks for dry ones, we tore open our packs, withdrew the socks, and felt the dry wool comfort absorb the clinging dampness of the English Channel. First to make the change was my Staff Sergeant, John Fisher. He walked up and down among our ten-man squad. He knew he had ten potential killers, and he didn't want any of them lagging behind because of pulling dry socks onto wet feet. We hiked toward the line of battle.

Opposite:
Warrior Statuette.
Cast bronze,
fifth-century BC.
Cincinnati Art Museum.
Gift of William Baer.

WHEN THE WAR ENDED, many of those who had participated had become civilians. It took several years for both large and small groups of veterans to form associations. In our case, B Company, Thirtieth Infantry Division, formed their own relatively small group. Every few years we met, always at a different city. First, there was West Point, then Sun City in Arizona, and then our fiftieth reunion in Traverse City, Michigan. Our company cook wrote to me to suggest we try to make contact with any members of the family of a former comrade of his who had been killed in Normandy. He suggested we invite them to our banquet, which would be the highlight of our reunion. I said I would try. Who was the man? I suddenly had goose bumps on my arms and legs. My scalp tightened. I couldn't talk for a moment.

The dead soldier's name was Staff Sergeant John Fisher.

I hadn't heard that name in fifty years!

Somewhere in Northern Michigan lived relatives of Johnny. Would they respond to an ad? An article? Another former sergeant, Ken Parker, knew his way around the newspaper business. He called the *Record-Eagle* in Traverse City and talked with the editor who agreed the information was well worth an announcement.

It appeared the next day, 1 June 1994. On June 2, two brothers of Sergeant Fisher called me at home in Virginia. On June 3, I received a call from Florence Fisher Oates, Johnny's wife. "Were you really with him when he . . ."

"Yes," I said. "I'll tell all his friends and relatives how it happened when I meet you in Traverse City." She told me that the Fisher family had been searching almost continuously for almost fifty years in an effort to discover just how Johnny had died.

Many of his closest relatives and parents had died, but what remained of his family, his nieces, nephews, and cousins, never lost hope. They began to call me in the next three days. My telephone number had been published with the article in the newspaper, so I had expected a few calls, but the phone never stopped ringing.

The meeting with the Fisher family took place in a second-floor conference room at two in the afternoon. I picked up my briefcase and started toward the door. My wife, feeling her presence might distract me, decided at that moment not to enter the room. Instead, she handed me a postcard-sized envelope, on the front was a prayer she had written asking for courage to tell the Fisher family how Johnny had spent his last minutes on earth. It was a wholesome prayer. When I read it at the beginning of my presentation, all distractions stopped. There was no whispering. Everyone was seated—waiting. To this day, I feel I may never have had the heart to tell them the truth of Johnny's death. The prayer gave me strength.

When Johnny's brothers told me not to expect any more than a dozen or so to attend, I felt that talking to such a small group would be most helpful. But, forty were waiting at the door to the conference room. My hands were sweating, as was my back—and my talk had not yet begun. Men with TV cameras wanted to record every word, but I said there couldn't be any cameras or recorders until after the meeting. They understood. I felt the need to keep such a presentation private. It was so personal an event: not something to be shared with the world. Later, several attendees thanked me for this policy. "This is a family matter," they said.

I stood at the head of the table. My guests had moved the chairs and grouped them much like a theater. I coughed and said "Good afternoon" and read the prayer "This is the most serious occasion in which I have ever participated. I like to feel that your Johnny would be doing this for me if our roles had been reversed. He died after our first forty days of combat when a tank-mounted eighty-eight cannon took his life. When he died along with another soldier, behind him, I didn't shed a tear. Instead, I was lying twenty feet to his left—with a smashed elbow and a perforated thigh. There wasn't time to blow your nose or scratch. There wasn't time to dig in, or throw a grenade. There wasn't time to check the breech in your rifle because, suddenly, we found ourselves among more of the enemy than we had ever seen!"

It was then I felt the tears welling up. No, not when I was in combat. I felt the tears coming when I was in that room with forty people I had never met before, and I knew if I shed tears then, the whole audience would be out of control doing what I would be doing; crying.

Every eye was watching me. For a few seconds I felt I might not be able to continue, but *I suddenly saw Johnny Fisher on a battlefield near Saint Jean. We had entered the town after artillery had destroyed everything in sight. His living face showed nothing other than a colossal alertness.* My mind stopped wandering, and I began my presentation.

Fisher had been promoted to Technical Sergeant—almost right after our landing on Omaha Beach—when Sergeant Weaver had been killed by a German rifleman on our first day of combat. I told how on the day Johnny died, machine guns from the Third Reich were showering the field we occupied. There were a hundred fifty U.S. soldiers in that field. Before another hour was gone there would be half that number still alive.

I ended by telling of the German tank splitting the turrets of the American tanks entering the field. Of the three smashed, the occupants of only one tank were left alive. The fourth tank made a run for it. The German tank was slightly above the field our tanks were in. The Americans didn't have a chance to see where the firing originated.

Seeing the fourth tank run for it, the Germans fired a last shot, hoping to kill the men backing out of the field. The shot missed. The shell hit a tree in front of Fisher. The shell was not fused to explode on contact, but to hit a tank, penetrate its armor plate, then explode. Instead, it penetrated the tree, continued to fly forward and, just as it would have behaved upon striking a tank, it exploded a microsecond after hitting the tree. Sergeant John Fisher was killed instantly. Another soldier, Jim Cash, was killed as the explosion propelled fragments in every direction.

I had been standing twenty feet to the left of Fisher. The explosion lifted me, tossing me into bushes on the hedgerow. And the war was over for three men in that field. I was the third casualty from that shell. I said to the Fishers that what they had heard from me was a true account of "How Johnny Died." I told them that I hadn't expected it to be so true-to-life. I firmly believe the ability of this ex-infantryman to address a gathering of forty strangers was enhanced by a heavenly power that was brought forth by prayer and the vivid appearance of Johnny's alive face. I had felt my strength increase after reading the prayer my wife had written. How else would someone, with little or no training, be able to speak to Johnny's friends and relatives on a subject so significant as this?

I finally said, "Now—you know."

I reached for my handkerchief. The audience was still. Why weren't they leaving? It was over. Then, a few at a time, they stood—and applauded.

Applause? That was too much. Then it was my turn to wipe away tears.

Later, the four brothers told me that, although fifty years had passed since the telegram arrived, there hadn't been a week they did not think about Johnny. How many families, I wondered, held silent vigils over the years, hoping for personal news of how their beloved had met death in a faraway place?

The late JAMES O. LOGAN wrote for publication for eighteen years after his retirement from the Bureau of National Affairs, Inc., Washington, D.C. His work appeared in the *Shenandoah Valley-Herald, Rural Living, Gleanings, Racing Pigeon Digest,* the *Northern Virginia Daily,* and other publications. He lived in Mount Jackson, Virginia.

PART III

The Shadow Side

like wide bolts
of fine Italian silk,
brilliant leaves
cover the small, still
pond from bank to bank
—ART STEIN

Without darkness, we really cannot understand light. . . . The evils we personally experience make us permanently opposed to certain kinds of evil. So the darkness in an individual's life brings about certain central eternal tendencies. The person who has lived through political leaders tearing up society for their own personal gain may forever be the one who externally treasures and promotes peace and cooperation between people.
—WILSON VAN DUSEN
The Design of Existence

VIRGIL SUÁREZ

Muñeca, Huntington Park, Nineteen Eighty Something

It was during the Summer Olympics
in Los Angeles that my father met her,
she came over with her then boyfriend
lover, some guy they called "Niño."

They called her Muñeca, which means
doll, and the three men at the party
swooned over her. My sister, mother,
and I watched these three grown

men outside on the lawn running
around her, the witch as we came
to know her. They smelled something
about her, as cats do, my mother

said. She promised never to have
any other parties—that was it, no more
free food and sangrias for that bitch.
A year later, my father left my mother

for Muñeca, who had left Niño
in what rumor held to be a pretty
ugly sight: clothes on the lawn, broken
windows, dented fender on the car.

Ugly. My father came home from work
one afternoon, told my mother like
he was saying goodbye to strangers,
got in the car and took off. I watched

from the living room window, across
the lawn as the car picked up speed
then turned for good at the corner.
I can't remember if my mother cried,

but we lived on, knowing that the gap
existed, and my mother and sister never
mentioned his name again. At night,
in the dark of my bedroom, I looked

at the picture of my mother and father
in Havana, outside the building where
they said they got married. And I thought
of Muñeca, how she had come that one

time and changed our lives forever.
Powder smooth cleavage and green
eyes, I remember how she tilted her neck
as she sipped sangria

to show off her chest. Her manicured
nails gripped and clicked against the glass.
And I promised myself I would remember
that Aren't-I-wonderful look,

the way she hissed words through her teeth.
Of course, her affair with my father lasted
only a couple of years. She left him like
my mother said she would, and my father

could never come back. The weakness of men,
my mother called it, for which he
would pay and pay and pay. He came by
every so often to say hello, or at school

to buy me and my sister lunch. Years later,
when my sister moved out, I went to college
in Florida. My mother stayed in California
and lived alone. My father died of a stroke.

Once in Miami at La Carreta, I was there
with my fiancee eating dinner, and I got up
to go to the bathroom, and to do so you have
to enter the cantina, a smoky dark cavern.

Muñeca sat at the bar working on her vermouth.
A man kept his head buried in her breasts.
He was drunk. She looked wasted, old and haggard.
The smoke of a burning cigar coiled in her hair.

I looked long enough to make sure it was she.
At that moment I thought of my father
and his friends that one afternoon on the lawn,
of my mother looking out at them, and she

now alone in her room in California,
the Spanish soap operas on the television,
watching as bad things happen to good people.
Me, I decided long ago not to get involved,

not to let these seeds take root
in the darkness of my memory.

VIRGIL SUÁREZ was born in Havana in 1962. He is the author of more than a dozen books, including, most recently, the poetry collections *Palm Crows, Banyan,* and *Guide to the Blue Tongue.* He lives in Key Biscayne and teaches at Florida State University in Tallahassee.

LAURA MUELLER

The First Day

Pablo Picasso.
Mother and Child.
Oil on canvas, 1901.
Fogg Art Museum, Harvard University Art Museums. Bequest from the Collection of Maurice Wertheim, Class of 1906.
©2002 Estate of Pablo Picasso/Artists Rights Society (ARS), New York.

SO MANY PEOPLE ARE TALKING ABOUT ANGER. I'm not there yet. My fear is like a black blanket wrapped so tightly around me that it's all I can see. Darkness, yes. Anger, no, not really, except for the fact that it happened on her first day. About that, I feel angry. About that, I am furious.

Yesterday morning, before the presence of darkness arrived, I spoke with a friend from a neighboring state. "I cried last night," she said. "I cried thinking of my baby, my big boy, going off to school."

"You did?" I didn't. I wondered if there was something wrong with me for not crying. I was full of many feelings about Sophie starting preschool, but I didn't feel like crying. Mostly, I was concerned that it would be a stupid school, a stupid experience, not nearly as rich as what I could provide for her at home. I was suffering from a superiority complex. And sure, I was sad, very sad. I have been with this child every day of her three and a half years. I'm the one who feeds her crackers and cream cheese, apple slices and milk. I'm the one who reads *Curious George Goes to the Hospital, Where the Wild Things Are,* and *Blueberries for Sal.* I'm the one who ties her shoes, reminds her to wash her hands, snaps her paint smock around her tender neck and then, with admiration for her work, tapes it to the wall. And I do it so well. Or so I like to think.

How will this be for Max, I wondered. Will he miss her? Will he enjoy the time without her? He'll have every baby to himself. He can push purple baby on the swing, put yellow baby to sleep under the rainbow silk blanket, and rock icicle baby in his arms singing "baah, baah black sheep" without his big sister running past him, stealing his treasure from the swing, its bed, his arms. Today, she won't be there to clutch the baby to her chest and croon to Max, "You can have this back, sweetie, when I'm done."

School starting means a lot of schlepping. I worry that Max will fall asleep in the car. That can't happen. That would be the worst thing that could possibly happen. If Max falls asleep in the car then he won't sleep at nap time. If he doesn't sleep at nap time, *I* won't get to sleep at nap time. No sleeping in the car. We'll get Sophie, go home, eat our macaroni and cheese and then sleep. It has to work like that.

She'll be hungry when I pick her up; thus she'll be grumpy. Grumpy leads to screamy. Her screams lead to mine. We must avoid this. Pack bread and cheese for the car ride home.

Worried, yes. Obsessive, oh yes. Tears, no.

Until, "Here we are Sweetie. Max and I will come in with you for a few minutes and then we're going to go."

"Okay."

She goes to the doll corner, picks up a baby, wraps it in a floral blanket, rocks it. Her little friend joins her, does the same with a fuzzy brown bunny and a blue flannel blanket. The girls put their babies in the cradle. They get out pots and pans, fill them with plastic carrots, onions, hot dogs, pizza slices, pineapples, and they cook.

She goes to the blocks, builds.

She goes to the easel, paints.

She goes to the speckled rug, reads.

"You're still here, Mommy?"

"Yes, well, Max is having such fun with the trucks. We're . . . we're leaving now."

And now my tears arrive. Oh, God no. Not here. Not now!

I kiss her and watch her sit on the speckled rug with the others. Her face glows, her yellow dress is smoothed down over that thin body. Little girl of mine. She is in school.

"Come, little boy. It's our special time now."

"Max want go walk in forest."

"Yes, let's go home and walk in the forest."

And we do. I can't sob for my baby who is not with us. I can't cry for what is over, gone, just like those orange curls she used to have. That's how it is with baby curls, cut them off and they are gone, just gone.

We sit in the forest while he eats his tamari sesame rice cake and his apple, which he carries in a small wicker basket with a handle. He takes a bite of rice cake, carefully places it back in the basket. He chews, takes out the apple, eats a tiny bite, places it in the basket. He climbs on a rotting birch log, pulls it apart a bit, picks me a giant fern, walks on. I follow. We do this for an hour-and-a-half. I am loving him, loving the non-interruptedness of him and me. I am not missing her. I am missing the baby she used to be, and that is what the quiet tears are about. I wipe them away and tell him it's time to go home.

The phone rings before I have a chance to take off my sneakers. I don't untie them first, this time. A roommate once told me that shoes last a lot longer if you untie them before you take them off, if you treat them gently. I always untie my shoes before I take them off. Today I don't.

It was Lisa on the phone, the mother of Sophie's little friend. The mother of the little girl who wrapped the brown fuzzy bunny in the blue flannel blanket.

"Laura, I'm calling because, well, I know you don't watch TV and, well, do you have any idea what's happening in the world right now?"

That feeling. That feeling that someone died. "What is it, Lisa?"

"New York City's been attacked. The World Trade Center is gone. Both buildings, they're gone. The Pentagon has been attacked. Airplanes have been hijacked, they're crashing into these buildings. New York City. Both World Trade Center buildings, gone, collapsed."

"What?" And she tells me what she knows and I cannot take it in. Max needs to pee. He uses the potty.

"Good job, Buddy. . . . I can't take this in, Lisa. It doesn't feel real. I don't understand."

She repeats what she knows, an hour after these attacks have happened. Again and again she tells me what she knows. I ask the same questions.

"Who's doing it? Both buildings? The Pentagon? How many people are . . ."

She tells, I ask. She tells, I ask.

"I just thought you should know," she says, "before you pick up Sophie, because everyone will be talking about it when the parents show up, and I thought you might want to just whisk her up and go."

"Yes, yes, good idea," I say, "so she doesn't have to feel any of this fear because, well, it's her first day of school and this day is supposed to be about her first day of school and I want it to be and . . . New York City? Manhattan? But how did they know how to fly a plane?"

Max and I drive to pick her up. He sits in Sophie's car seat instead of his own. A big treat. I sneak snippets of the radio. I don't want Max to pick up on this. This has nothing to do with him. Nothing.

". . . and the stock market is . . . closed!" the reporter says with something in his voice that reminds me of hysteria.

I am the first parent to arrive. It is obvious that the teachers and the two mothers who stayed all morning know nothing about this. It is a relief that they know nothing about this. I shake it away, the black blanket that tries to wrap itself around me.

No! Not here. Go! You can come back later, you can be sure, but not now.

Sophie is climbing a tree; others are digging in the sand box. Two children are playing on the seesaw which is in the shape of an airplane. An airplane.

The blanket returns.

Go away!

The teachers are watching, on duty, guarding, keeping the children safe.

I said go! Later, come back later.

"How was it? How'd she do?" I ask. I watch my child run to her little friend, grab her hands, twirl.

"She did great. She painted a picture, helped fix snacks. She has a great ability to take breaks from the stimulation. She just curled up a couple of times on the little couch and looked at books. It was really amazing that she could renew herself like that."

Yes, I think, she is amazing. Yes, I know this about her. I know her. So well.

"Hi baby," I say, looking up at her back in the tree she just climbed.

"I don't want to go," she says. And I know she has had a great time, that she is ready for this, that this is good.

I see the two mothers who stayed all morning. I know they are both from New York. I don't tell them. I see the teacher who is smiling at my daughter. I know that he fought in Vietnam. I don't tell him. I thank the teachers, take my daughter, go home.

"Did you feel like a brave girl, Sophie? Going to your first day of school?"

"I didn't feel like a brave girl, Mommy. I felt like a scared girl."

"Yes," I say. "I understand. You felt like a scared girl. That makes sense." Am I saying the right thing? I think that's the right thing.

I give the children lunch. I put Max to bed by himself. We have tried napping with Max but he needs to talk, dance, sing, play, sometimes for as long as an hour before he falls asleep. I climb into Sophie's bed with her.

I am falling apart. Images are coming back. But . . . how did they know how to fly a plane? I am losing it.

The black blanket arrives. Around and around it covers me up. "You said I could come back. Here I am."

Yes. Here you are. I have to say something. Something.

"Sophie." We are under her blue and green quilt that her father and I made for her when she left our bed. "I'm feeling sad today because some people died."

"When did this happen?"

"This morning."

Silence. I will give no more information than that. This is not about her, but I needed to say something, my grief so close to her pillow. She talks again.

"This morning, Mommy? They died this morning?"

"Yes, honey."

"Well . . . are you used to it yet?"

"No, baby, not yet."

And that's it, isn't it? Getting used to it. And I will be, we all will be. It will be what happened. It *will* be what happened, but it isn't right now. Right now it's what's happening, and it happened on her first day.

LAURA MUELLER lives in southern Vermont where she currently says to herself (many times a day), "I am practicing non-attachment." This story is her first published piece.

JONATHAN FRY

Butterflies and Hurricanes

On some remote corner of the universe, poured out and glittering in innumerable solar systems, there once was a star on which clever animals invented knowledge. That was the haughtiest and most mendacious minute of 'world history'—yet only one minute. After nature had drawn a few breaths the star grew cold, and the clever animals had to die.

—FREIDRICH NIETZSCHE

EVER SO SILENTLY a moth descended upon the screen door to rest before it would take flight again to fulfill its nightly toils. July's hum of crickets and katydids filled the twilight air, and the wind chimes on the front porch created a frantic dance of tangled strings. It had been nearly thirty-three long almanac years since Samuel McDowell had returned from the war, and he was living proof that time did not heal all wounds. He readjusted himself in his favorite rocking chair and awaited the coming storm.

A look of contentment polished Sam's wrinkled, leathery face as he sat there in his overalls and green John Deere hat, pumping back and forth in a fluid motion. He recalled an old saying that his father had used to explain how weather, and life for that matter, were predictably unpredictable. He'd called it, 'The Butterfly Effect', the theory that a butterfly flapping its wings in China today could cause a main-scale hurricane in Florida a week later. It was a name given to the undeniable effects that minuscule, trivial things have on the outcome and direction of much greater events. Along those same lines one could attempt to justify certain events that would occur in life.

Lightning flickered off in the distance and Sam counted aloud. "One Mississippi . . . two Mississippi . . . three Mississippi . . . four Miss-" *crack!* "Won't be long now," he murmured to whatever cowering creatures might be listening. Within the rolling of the minutes into hours and hours into weeks and weeks into years and so on throughout life, major events transpired that, in retrospect, appear nothing more than a sum of a few lesser and, at the time, seemingly insignificant happenings. It was within this specific framework of thinking in which Sam was transfixed while he methodically worked the rocking chair and awaited the storm.

Droves of flies and moths clung in desperation to the screen door for fear of being swept away in the wind. The door opened, and panic erupted as insects burst into flight, carried away in a swirl of wind. What little light there was revealed a tall young man in his early twenties. He sported heavily stained jeans, a worn, once-white, "Swiss-cheese" tank top, and held a fly swatter in his left hand. He instinctively adjusted his grease-stained red ball cap and seated himself in the chair beside Sam. For awhile no words were exchanged between the two as they stared off toward the increasingly violent flashes of lightning above the mountain looming in the distance.

Sam couldn't help but be proud of the young man he saw sitting before him—a protégé of Sam himself—only without so many of the rough edges. He was making his way through college, thanks to Sam and some loans, and would soon graduate with a degree in psychology and philosophy.

It was the boy who would break the silence first.

"Dad," began the young man, "how did this happen? I mean, why wouldn't they pay for your treatment?"

Sam flashed a crooked smile his son's way and started laughing which, as it always did these days, ended in a terrible fit of coughing. "Well, Jer, I'm sure I don't know. Ain't gonna sit here and pretend to neither."

"Come on old man," taunted Jer, cuffing his father on the head with a fly swatter, "you may look like a dumb hick, but you always have something in the pressure cooker." He swatted as if to strike his father in the head again.

"OK, I guess me ruse don't work on ye no more boy," said Sam in his dead give-away Irish accent. There was a slight pause and then he continued, "Do ye remember how pappy used to talk about 'The Butterfly Effect'?"

Jer nodded in recollection.

"Well, I been thinkin' about it and tryin' to trace everythin' that's been goin' bad lately to that one small incident that started it all." Sam continued.

Jer looked intrigued; his father could weave one hell of a story. "And?" he said impatiently.

"And I think I know what it was." replied Sam matter-of-factly.

Rain started pelting down periodically, making craters in the dust below the porch. Faster and faster it came on. The wind increased, and the chimes' frantic dance became a twisted, violent display of entangled strings.

Lightning flashed nearby. In union, Jer and Sam began to count, "One Mis-" *boom!* The thunder was so loud it rattled Sam's dentures.

"Let's wait till she dies down and don't holler!" shouted Sam. Jer nodded, and together they waited for the storm to subside.

While the storm drowned out all the other noises around them, Sam wondered what kind of side effects his illness was having on his son. Jer picked up his own stoic demeanor when it came to such matters, and it was difficult to get a feel for just how Jer was handling all this.

Eventually the rain slowed its earthly descent to a steady, soaking drizzle. The lightning and thunder passed. Finally, Sam cleared his throat loudly and began to speak again. "The way I see it," he began, "when I was a lad 'bout eight or ten years after pappy moved us here from Irelan', I had a chance to go to college. Now at the time, I grew up in a lower-class family, so I couldn't expect any help from them as far as financin' me education went. So a few months before the whole Vietnam fiasco started, I decided on gettin' me a job at ol' Shelton's store. All required was stock shelves, mop, repair things, and any other not-so-pleasant task that needed doin'. I was only makin' minimum, but I figured all I needed to do was save up for a few months, and I'd have enough for my first semester at junior college." Sam started coughing in great uncontrollable heaves, which

Cat Bootscraper. Cast iron, 11⅜×17½×3 in., ca. 1900. The American Folk Art Museum, New York. Gift of the Friends Committee of the Museum of American Folk Art. 1979.22.1.

ended in a loud snort followed by a large quantity of mucous promptly being hurtled over the porch fence.

"Where was we? Oh yeah, anyways, pop used to lend me the truck now and again so I wouldn't have to bike on down to Shelton's store. I was a wee bit late and was haulin' a good deal o'er the local speed limit. As I came up the top o' Millerstown Hill, there was a cat right smack dab in the middle o' the flamin' road. Lookin' back at that moment now, I know I shoulda just run o'er the damn thing, but as first instinct would dictate, I swerved to avoid it and sent pop's truck crashin' down o'er the hill and into a big ol' chestnut tree. Now, mind ye, neither I nor the cat were injured. Pop's truck had seen its last day though, and I would spend the remainder of that summer workin' to help him get a new one." Sam chuckled. "I once heard someone define 'irony' as an outcome of events contrary to what was, or what might have been, expected. I think 'irony' and 'The Butterfly Effect' are probably best buds lookin' down at me and laughin' real good right about now."

Jer was smiling; he found it interesting to listen to his father's unique blend of backwoods grammar and well-read intelligent "bookly" words. Just when you thought he was a complete hick, he would throw some amazingly obscure word out that would hint at intelligence far beyond what his manner and appearance suggested.

The storm had all but passed. The crickets and katydids cautiously started on their serenade of the summer, as soft pillows of fog gently rolled in from the mountains. The trees began their drip-drying process.

"I often wondered what made that cat sit there right in the road at that specific time," Sam continued, while puffing greedily at his freshly packed pipe, "probably . . . a butterfly for all I know . . ."

Jer leaned forward in his seat and swatted a June bug. "That story is a little melodramatic for you dad."

"I'm not done yet, boy!" hollered Sam, causing a few coughs from deep within his mucous-filled throat. "Due to the fact that I had to spend me summer workin' to help pop get a new truck, I was unable to attend college that fall for lack o' money. As fate, or in this case, the butterfly, would have it, that was the year that they started draftin' for 'Nam. I was one o' the first to get called. Now keep in mind that if ye were in college ye were 'exempt' from bein' drafted, sort of a 'shield' which some folks tried to hide behind."

Jer nodded, beginning to see where his father's story was headed.

Sam took a long draw from his pipe and spoke again. "I probably don't need to recite the details o' the war to ye, but it had a life changin' impact on me. Most important was that the government used a herbicide called 'Agent Orange' which was designed to kill the jungle vegetation. They would load planes full o' this poison and dump it o'er miles o' rainforest. Some days we would be as soaked from the Agent Orange as we were from blood and rain."

Sam paused and shook as if a chill had caught him. Probably some memory of the war had just sent the willies up his spine, thought Jer.

"Well, years after the war, ye was just a young tike, I was diagnosed with a form of cancer called Hodgkin's disease. There had been studies done proving that people exposed to Agent Orange developed this sort of side effect. So I had to have radiation treatments in hopes of silencin' the disease and prolongin' me life."

"Which the government compensated you for," interrupted Jer.

"Yes, they compensate me for the radiation treatment. But now, twenty years after the treatment I have developed a slew o' health problems—the worst o' these bein' me bad heart, which the doctors tell me is a direct result of the radiation treatment. It weakened me heart, boy. Ye tell me how the government is supposed to 'compensate' me for that?"

Sam seemed suddenly bitter. He stood up as if to leave, but then leaned against the porch fence and continued with his story.

"This here heart," Sam thumped a gnarled fist into his chest, "is gonna fail me before too long, boy. Now let's do some imagining and try to predict the ramifications that my death will have on the world."

Jer laughed aloud and repeated the word 'ramifications' as if to mock his father.

"So let's pretend that tomorrow I die," Sam said, sitting down in his chair again, "how would ye feel? Would you hold ill will toward the U.S. government?"

Jer nodded his agreement, "Damn right I would. I already hold ill will for the government. That would just intensify it."

"All right then. Now let's suppose that after I'm dead the government raises property taxes so high that ye can't afford to keep the house and land that I left ye in my will. Ye're already angry with them 'cause they caused the premature death o'yer father. So let's just suppose that all these things combine to cause a momentary loss of sanity and durin' this loss o' sanity ye somehow kill the president." Sam said in a rising voice not unlike a TV evangelist: "Durin' the vice president's rise to power, a terrorist organization sees an openin' to steal some o' our nuclear weapons . . . and succeeds. Later on that week the terrorists launch their newly acquired toys at the U.S. and a full blown nuclear war ensues. A few days later the world as we know it is completely destroyed."

A gust of wind slithered in across the pine trees and tickled the chimes. "Yeah, dad, nice story. But I don't think I'll ever kill anyone, let alone assassinate the president. Do you actually think that something that drastic is a direct result of that cat being in your way?" Jer said.

"Hell yes! Look at what I'm tellin' ye boy! Never once when I was young did I think I'd kill anyone neither till there was people shootin' at me. I bet if I told ye ye'll die at age fifty-four of a bad heart, ye'd probably think there was a snowball's chance o' that happenin', too. Yet, look at me! If not for that blasted flea-bitten feline, I'd be just passin' me prime right now instead o' knockin' on death's door!"

I guess so . . ." Jer said while he adjusted his ball cap.

"So in short, 'The Butterfly Effect', which is gonna cause me death, is the fact that the damned cat had to be in that damned road at the damned time. And, if ye'r not careful, me boy, ye may just cause the end o' the world."

Jer burst into laughter, "Or for all you know," Jer said, "maybe the cat that caused all of this will end up being the spark that starts the creative engine in my head. Perhaps someday I will write a story about the 'The Butterfly Effect' that will revolutionize the way people see the world and bring about world peace and end world hunger."

They each erupted in laughter. "Yes! Yes!" bellowed Sam between laughs and coughs. "I think ye could be right! O' course, I'd be wagering me wallet on ye bein' the assassinator and not the writer!"

This last remark prompted a fly swatter being flung in the direction of Sam, who deftly raised a hand and caught it in midair. A tug-of-war ensued which saw the fly swatter broken in two.

They laughed a little while more, and then everything grew still. The rain had stopped, but off in the distance the sound of thunder rolling over the hills was nearly drowned out by the chorus of night-time insects.

"Simpsons are on in ten minutes," Sam winked.

"I'll make the popcorn," Jer smiled.

"Meet ye in the livin' room in five minutes!" Sam said rising from his chair.

They swung the screen door open and walked into the house, all but oblivious as a startled moth took flight into the night air.

JONATHAN FRY recently graduated from the University of Pittsburgh, "where," he writes, "I studied philosophy and learned how to think analytically about being unemployed." He writes poetry and short stories but hopes to tackle his first novel soon. In his free time, Fry enjoys chess, basketball, reading, skateboarding, classical music, punk-rock music, and screening his phone calls.

DOROTHY HOWE BROOKS

Half-Life

I.

That invisible spark,
bundle of radiant energy
released as one atom transforms,
laser-sharp, brilliant
as a shooting star,
then gone.
Chance selection, yet
one atom's decay
preserves the rest.

II.

Boys will defy—
they will hang from pitons,
dive into murky water,
trespass on footbridges—
they dare their immortal bodies
to fail them.

We can't save them all.
One or two slip,
their bodies radiating
all that youthful energy
in one splendid burst,
burnt offering
to the god of fickle chance.

We can't save them. Yet they,
by their going, save us.

DOROTHY HOWE BROOKS enjoys sailing the coastal waters of the Gulf with her husband. Her poetry and short fiction have appeared or are forthcoming in *Slant: A Journal of Poetry, REAL: Re Arts and Letters, Sojourner, Eureka, The Georgia Journal,* and *The Habersham Review.* Her work has also appeared in the anthology *If I Had My Life to Live Over, I Would Pick More Daisies* (1992). Author of *Simple Facture* (1995), a chapbook, Dorothy is currently at work on a novel.

PAULA DONAGHY

Foggy Night

SHE WALKED THE BIG DOG on a short leash with frequent tugs and calls to heel. On her right, down the long drive and east of the dunes, the March ocean grumbled to itself. The iron-gray winter water had conjured up dense fog that filled the starless night with mysterious striations. She lifted her eyes to the place in the northern sky where the comet had been. *Hale-Bop, what sights had that celestial traveler seen circling the solar system every two thousand years,* she wondered. She tugged the leash "Heel, Chance." The shepherd looked back at her, beyond her, pricked his ears at something behind her, didn't growl, hackles down, no tail wag, just curious. The back of her neck tingled, moist fingers of fog stroked her face, slowly she turned.

Outlined in the muted glow from the old fire station across the street was an animal, a dog? He sat straight on the sidewalk, paws primly together, ears up, waiting. She sensed shining eyes, an almost smiling mouth. Ghostly gray, he seemed haloed in the damp light. *Odd,* she thought, *whose dog is that? What dog is that? Is that a dog?* She recalled the soul-seeking eyes of a red wolf newly mended at the vet's, the resigned eyes of a dying pelican she'd watched with on the beach, the round wary eyes of a harbor seal in rehab at the aquarium, the frozen eyes of a deer caught in the lateral wash of her headlights on another foggy night. *I've got to spend more time with people,* she thought, giving herself a mental shake. The fog grew thicker around her, the light continued to halo the animal like some Kirlian aura. As she turned and walked on toward the hidden comet, she added *wild* to the sense of soul-seeking eyes and smiling mouth. Her dog stayed close, the leash slack as she walked a little faster wondering if the creature would follow. All sound was muffled in the mist. She doubted that this animal would make sounds even on dry pavement, wondered if its feet even touched the ground.

Opposite:
Romaine Brooks.
Self-Portrait.
Oil on canvas, 1923.
Smithsonian American
Art Museum.
Gift of the artist.

Thoughts of the comet were replaced by speculation. *Maybe a fox.* There had been a gray fox even before they built the house. He'd marked the drive every day, a little pile of berry-filled scat at the end and strong urine on the turnaround. She'd seen him once trotting into the brush across the road in the early morning mist. For years there had been that pile, that scent, tracks across the dunes, down beside the house. "This place is mine" they said, "I was here first, when there were no dunes, when the ocean swept freely across this island. I was here when inlets opened and closed as easily as doors, and whales washed up on the beach to feed my whole family for a year. Now you build your house on my trail. Fool!"

She walked now in a small bubble of sight. Distance was distorted by the fog. She became disoriented, had she walked a mile? Ten? An hour? A day? A year? As she turned toward home, the dog snorted, ears up hesitating, then stretched out his front legs, rump up, head between his paws in that "let's play" pose. She knew before she saw, that the creature was still there watching, waiting. *What kindred spirit are you?* Kindred it was, there was no doubt. As she moved back toward it, the animal darted into the brush beside the walk. When she hurried on, she sensed rather than saw, a shadow moving ahead of her until she actually saw it move across the street into the uncivilized terrain behind the old station and vanish. "Oh" she moaned, and a sense of loss, of miracles unseen, chances not taken, filled her with a terrible loneliness.

She reached the long driveway, turned toward the muttering of the March Atlantic, and trudged, only human, an old lady with her dog, up the steps to her empty house.

PAULA DONAGHY lives on the Outer Banks off the coast of North Carolina. She has been writing for more than forty years, has received the Dare County Silver Arts Award, has been a member of the Dare County Writer's Group, and considers herself a storyteller. As the volunteer coordinator for the North Carolina Aquarium on Roanoke Island, she writes and publishes its monthly newsletter.

PART IV

Fate or Chance?

an ice storm
coats the maple trunks
the glitter
and shadows unreal
full sap moon
—Art Stein

. . . many people take the whole of existence as simply physical. This assumption is understandable since it is the material world we know best. Present-day cosmology, which attempts to stretch the material world to explain everything, is limited to the four-dimensional, space-time material world. But, in trying to explain our conscious experience and even more so in explaining levels approaching God, the four-dimensional material world is simply too limited.
—Wilson Van Dusen
The Design of Existence

Telechron

PAUL F. WOLF

Tunnels of Light

WE PULLED OFF THE HIGHWAY into a convenience store–service station, and as I filled the car with gas, Dorothy went inside to buy a package of cigarettes. While I pumped the fuel, snow piled on my gloves and covered the back window; it was heaving itself towards the ground at a rate that would bury the entire state of Wisconsin in a matter of hours. It can't last, I thought, a storm this hard will blow away in about half an hour. Still, the pink glowing of light from the overhead lamps was blurred, as if from a sandstorm, and I could barely see the inside of the store where Dorothy was buying her smokes. I pulled the nozzle out, placed the cap back on the gas-fill, walked the hose to the machine, then headed inside to warm up.

"You look like a snowman," Dorothy said when I stepped in.

I patted my hands together. "Feel like one, too," I said. I noticed a girl behind the counter, heard the sounds of a TV. "What's the weatherman say?" I asked.

"It'll keep up all night," the girl answered.

"Can't," I said.

"Yes, it can," Dorothy cut back. We were coming from Chicago but she was a Wisconsin native and spoke with the authority of experience. "Today," I said, "is the first day of spring."

"It can," Dorothy said again.

"It comes in off the lake," the girl told me. "It hits, blows back out, then back in again. There's a motel right up the road."

"Should we take it, Dan?" Dorothy asked.

"No," I said. "Why stop for a little snow?"

On the way back to the car it seemed to be coming down even harder. Our boots crunched, and it was the only sound in what seemed like an unearthly, speckled silence.

◆

Opposite:
Robert Rauschenberg.
Reservoir.
Oil, pencil, fabric, wood and metal on canvas, 1961. Smithsonian American Art Museum. Gift of S.C. Johnson & Son, Inc.

SOME PEOPLE COVER THEIR PAIN with loud, boisterous voices. Others haul it around in silence, even though you can still see it, sense it, feel the moroseness that has touched their lives. Dorothy hid hers, dealt with it by being agreeable, warm, trying to please everyone she cared about so they would never see what was hovering inside. But it was there, throbbing like a knife-slash. We'd met at A.A., and along with her deep belief in a higher power, she'd decided to confront things, like a gun fighter in an old Western. For Dorothy, the bad guy was her alcoholic mom, and the town was a place called Henryville, Wisconsin. I thought she was carrying it too far, both the religious part and the showdown with her mom, but we'd gotten involved just a few months before, so to keep the peace, I decided to go along. But there was really a lot more at stake for me than that—I cared for her more deeply than I'd felt for anyone in a long time, and I was hoping for something more to develop than just a casual affair. But I still had my doubts about Henryville; even more about her need to worship with the simplicity of a child.

"You're thirty-seven," I said as we drove. "That stuff happened when you were in high school."

"I'm not going to bring all that up. I haven't seen her in over three years. And I owe her an apology."

"I'd think she owed you one."

"Maybe so. But I have to feel right about myself."

"She was a good woman to run away from, if you ask me." Her mother would try to seduce Dorothy's boyfriends, show up drunk at PTA meetings, pass out in church, have flings with married men she'd pick up in local bars.

"I just need to tell her I'm sorry."

"I bet she won't even remember it."

"Of course she will. And what I did was wrong."

Her mother had shown up at Dorothy's apartment in Chicago, drunk, banging on the door, yelling, begging to get in. Dorothy had peeked out, stared, then slammed the door in her face. She hadn't seen her since. It was that episode which had caused Dorothy to make the decision to straighten out her life.

"Maybe we should have stopped at that motel," she said.

"You're changing the subject."

"I can hardly see the road."

"We'll get through," I said. "It covers the pavement, but the wind blows it off, so it's not always that deep."

We got to an Interstate, and as I inched along, Dorothy walked in front of the car, tapping through the snow with the sharp tip of an umbrella. The stuff had washed over the road, and since no other cars had come by before us, it was like looking at an ocean of white—she had to keep us on track by striking the concrete. I honked and she ran back and jumped in, breathing hard.

She looked healthy, her face pink, eyes darting around, a smile crossing her lips. It was hard to imagine how she'd described herself in the past: bloated, eyes squinty, laced with red, slurring her words, waking up in hallways, or on El trains at the end of the line.

She'd gotten involved with cocaine, starting with a few sniffs and ending up on crack. She'd alluded to life on the streets, after her career in nursing had gone away. I couldn't picture her a hooker and I never asked, but I was aware how far they'd go when they needed their stuff. "The meetings saved my life," she often claimed. "I'd drink or smoke anything in front of me."

"I can see a little better now," I said as she settled into the car. "But I'll go out next, if we have to."

She laughed. "This is so bad, it's almost good."

I pushed on the gas. Every few seconds the wind brushed away a path and I got a peek at the pavement. I admired Dorothy's spirit; as for getting involved, I had no regrets. We'd both felt an attraction at the meetings, breaking the rules and trading last names. But now she seemed to be holding back.

"This could be dangerous, Dan," she said, tapping the snow off her boots.

"What could be dangerous? The snow, your mother, or us?"

She laughed. "All of it, I guess." Then: "Yes. Us. I do have concerns, you know? And the storm! And my mother!"

"I love the storm," I said. "And this engine. Twin cams, sixteen valves, fuel injection. This is fun. I can drive through anything. Man against nature!"

"Oh brother," she said, playfully. "Next you're going to say it's metaphysical."

THE TRUCK HAD JACKKNIFED ON THE ICE and skidded about a hundred feet, hit an exit sign, then in a shower of splintered debris, turned on its side and plowed off the road. We arrived on the scene a few minutes after it happened and it was the truck driver who told us the story. A few other cars had stopped and we all stood by the side of the vehicle as the snow kept falling and the phosphorescent light of the flares made our faces look apparitional in the night.

"I'm lucky I'm alive," the guy said.

"You're right," I answered.

"That wind came out like a big hand and just shoved me down."

The cab of the truck was crumpled on the passenger side, the seat thrown out and lying in the snow. He had a long, bleeding slash on his arm and the blood seemed to come from the tattoo of a rose etched in his skin. His coat must have still been in the cab.

"I take my wife with me sometimes," he said. "If she'd been in there, she'd be gone."

Then Dorothy was next to him, throwing a sweater over his shoulders. "Here," she said.

"Thanks." He seemed dazed, as though he didn't really know what had taken place.

"Will the police come?" someone asked.

"How will they even know it happened?" I said.

"They must patrol. This is an Interstate highway."

"But in this weather?" someone else answered. "Who knows when a cop will come by?"

We all looked around as if we were stranded in a desert. "Hey," a woman said. "There's a farmhouse out there!"

In the distance we could see a light, about a half-mile off, as if someone had a lantern burning in a dense bank of fog.

The driver glanced at the small crowd. "Listen," he said. "This road is like death. I'm walking to that farm."

"So are we," said a woman. She looked at the man who was with her. "Just leave the car, Ed. We'd be crazy to keep driving."

"Let's go then," said the driver. "I'm sure they'll let us get some sleep."

The whole group started trudging away, but I didn't follow, staying pinned in my tracks.

"Do you still think this is fun?" Dorothy asked.

"They're doing the safe thing," I answered. "But something is telling me we should keep driving."

She hesitated before she spoke. "You heard what the driver said," she told me, at last.

"I know. But we've done okay so far. And I've got a feeling."

"I'm not so sure about that feeling," she said. "But I guess I'm with you."

I'D BEEN IN THE ARMY FOR FOUR YEARS, STATIONED OVERSEAS. The barracks was a regular junk house: heroine, crack, grass, hash, any kind of booze. That's how I started, first on wine, then grass, a little toot, whiskey, then mostly just beer and smoke when I got out. I managed to hold on to my job as a sales rep and never thought of myself as a junkie or a drunk, but that's what they all say. I tried AA because nothing else had worked; it was hard listening to the higher power bit, but some people said the program made you quit, so what did I have to lose? Dorothy was a devoted Christian, and I had to admit she was a big help. Just as I'd never seen her stoned, she'd never seen me. Wanting to keep it that way was often what kept me going.

"I don't blame the army," I told her as we drove. The remark came out of nowhere, almost like the storm had brewed it, but I knew she'd catch on right off. It was always on your mind, like a nagging cold.

"I know," she said.

Outside the car, snow was beating down as if the sky were spitting at us just to block our way. Every once in a while, I'd get out and shovel a drift off the road so we could get through. By then we were three hundred miles out of Chicago, a hundred left to go. I was starting to get tired, but would never let myself say I'd been whipped.

WE HAD TO CUT OFF THE INTERSTATE and begin taking a series of two-lane roads. We got to some small towns, the houses dark, no motels, the only thing open being the bars. Snowmobiles cut back and forth across the streets; a few of the drivers waved: camaraderie in ice.

We stopped in one of the taverns to order some coffee.

"How far is Henryville?" I asked the bartender.

"It's a good sixty miles. You're not driving are you?"

"Yeah," I said. "We are."

"It's letting up a bit," he said. "But it's still pretty rough."

"We did real good in there," I said to her, once we were back in the car and moving again.

"Yes," she said. "We did."

"How close were you?"

"Not too far," she said. "But you see, I wasn't alone."

"Do you mean me or something *divine*?" I asked. I tolerated what Dorothy believed, as long as it made her feel at peace. But there were times she seemed to push it into everything, and it often made me ill at ease. And I knew my views irritated her.

"I was thinking of God," she said.

"Well think of me," I answered. "After all, I'm driving."

About then was when I looked up and saw two tunnels of light in the sky somewhere ahead; they pierced the darkness and bore through the snow-drenched air, as if aimed by some huge device that wanted to brighten the night. I pointed them out to Dorothy. "I wonder what they could be?" I asked.

"I don't know."

"Well, they're right on our way, whatever they are. We'll be getting there in no time at all."

LIKE A MIRAGE ON A SUN-BLEACHED HIGHWAY, the longer we drove, the less we seemed to gain on them. We were able to drive a little faster by then, even though we had to keep watching for drifts that would appear as we crested a hill. Once I skidded into a heap and we had to stop and gouge our way out. But we kept going, and what I began to notice was that Dorothy hardly questioned me, never seemed to wonder why I had to keep driving on. That worried me. I knew she wanted to stop, but was keeping her aggravation inside.

"Maybe it's a signal of some kind," I said.

"Or a sign," she answered. "It's a shame you don't believe, Dan."

"I'm a confirmed atheist. Always was and always will be."

She frowned, didn't answer.

"But I'm an atheist with a heart. Got to like that, don't you?"

"The part about the heart I can handle," she said.

"Well, let's not get into it right now, okay? It's a pair of spotlights or something. Like when they open up a new store."

She turned her head. "A store? Now? It's midnight."

"You're right," I answered. "A strange time for an opening."

In an odd sort of way, the lights guided us. They pulled at us and gave us a sense of direction, as if someone were leading us along our way. Enigmatic, we found comfort in them, like a powerful will was telling us that to keep going was the right thing to do. Finally, as the snow fell yet harder once more, as the piles and heaps began to get worse yet again, the tunnels began to get closer until it seemed they were just over the next rise.

When we pulled up to them, there was no resolution, no moment of enlightenment. We saw a huge mound of snow off the downslope of the road, then the luminescence shooting from a gaping hole in the top of the pile, as if someone had placed giant lamps into an unfinished grave.

"This doesn't make sense," Dorothy said, as we stared.

It took me about a minute to reason it out. "Yes it does," I called. "Get the shovel out of the trunk!"

We climbed up and through the protrusion of white, slipping, falling in past our knees, tramping ahead. The wind had picked up and by the time we got to the top, it felt like the tips of my fingers had been cut off. "Lord," said Dorothy.

The vehicle was buried about four feet below the opening on the surface, front end up, standing perpendicular on its hind end. Someone was in the driver's seat, trapped by the snow sheathed tightly around the body of the car. A weakly moving pair of hands motioned at us, then fell still. We started to shovel, pacing ourselves. I took a turn, Dorothy took a turn, the idea being to dig a path to the driver's door so we could get it open and pull out whoever was inside. When we got deeper, I had to fill the shovel with snow, then pass it up to Dorothy so she could empty it and pass it back to me for refilling. Under we went, like moles, until about twenty minutes later I was able to leverage the door open about a foot and a half.

"Thank God," a woman's voice said from inside.

I reached in and grabbed at her left shoulder, sliding her towards our cave. After a moment, she seemed able to muster some of the power she needed herself. "Thank God," she said again. When I had her free, Dorothy reached across and we were able to get her to the top of the heap of snow. We didn't talk again until we were in the car and the heater was pumping warmth all over her.

"I was trapped," she said. "I had the heater on, but then it ran out of gas. I just hoped someone would see the lights before the battery went dead."

"How did you get in there?"

"I don't know. I skidded and then it went up in the air, into the snow." She sputtered out a cough, then breathed in and let out a sigh.

"But you're okay now," Dorothy said. "Praise the Lord."

"Yes," she said. "Praise the Lord. I'm Nancy, by the way."

NANCY TALKED US INTO STAYING AT HER PLACE in the next town.She told us we were only a few miles from Henryville, but we decided to stop anyway. We made coffee and got a fire going, but after only a few minutes Nancy said she was tired and thought she should go to bed. "It's going to feel good to cuddle in," she told us. "Help yourselves if you need a drink." Then Dorothy and I were alone by the fire.

"I wonder what her story is?" I asked, my voice quiet.

"I don't know. She can't be over thirty. But this is a great house." The living room had cathedral ceilings, a large kitchen just behind, a balcony overlooking from above, and she'd told us we had our own bedroom and bath. The fully stocked bar was near the fireplace.

"By small-town, Wisconsin standards," Dorothy said, "this place is a palace."

"A night full of mystery," I said. "And we won't be needing that bar, will we?"

"I know that," she said, then: "She could have died in that car if we hadn't come along. You're aware of that, too, aren't you?"

"Yes, I am."

"And you still don't believe in a spiritual being?"

I put my arm around her shoulder. "No, I don't. Can't you just respect that without always trying to convert me?"

She didn't answer. I knew my lack of religion ate at her, especially at a moment like this. It would all seem to fit together, make a perfect parable, add sense to my seemingly irrational need to keep heading north all night. But I wouldn't give an inch.

"Look," I said. "I'm a decent man. I helped save the woman in the car. I got off the booze. If we stick together, we'll both get straight. I'm a strong man, Dorothy. I'll get you past your mother tomorrow like I got us through the storm. Isn't all that enough?"

She moved away from me on the couch so that my arm fell from her shoulder. "I always told myself I could never get serious with a man who wasn't a Christian," she said.

"And that's so important to you? Just that?"

"I think it is, Dan. I really do."

"You're not supposed to judge, are you? In your religion? But isn't that just what you're doing? Judging the hell out of me?"

"And the fact that you had to keep driving? A coincidence?"

"Why not? Why does it always have to follow a plan or some form of divine providence? Why can't things just happen?"

She stood up and looked down at me. "I guess it's all in your point of view, isn't it!"

I stood up, too, facing her, my face flushed. "No. That's not what it is at all. What this is about is your intolerance, which is more dangerous to have floating around than what a million atheists think about the creation of the world!"

"It's not intolerance! I'm not some bigot! Faith is just a very important thing to share."

"Is it? Think about two people. Think of all the things they don't share. Jobs. Certain interests. Certain friends. A thing is only crucial if you have it in your mind that you can't work around it."

I reached to her, but she pulled away. "Can't you just accept what I believe?" I said.

"That's a difficult thing to ask, Dan. It really is."

I pondered for a while, watching the flames dance in front of me, like magic answers. But they were, after all, only flames.

"I was starting to think we were going somewhere," I told her.

She was staring at the fireplace, too. "Maybe we were," she said. "Or maybe it's just that we fit together now, at this precise moment in time. Who knows how we'll feel next year?"

I tapped a log in the fire with the tip of my boot. "I feel good about us. I think that's all the assurance a person can ever expect. You just take how you feel, and go with it."

"You make it sound so simple," she said.

I reached for her again, and this time she let me give her a little squeeze. "One's faith means a lot," she said.

"What about love?"

She stepped towards the bay window that looked out towards the road. Snow was still falling. I could see her reflection in the glass like two of her standing in the room. "I've been known to change my mind about things," she said quietly.

I stepped up behind her and kissed her lightly on her neck.

"Good," I said. All of the anger in the room seemed to seep away and disappear, as if pulled out into the cold of the night.

"Everything can get so complicated, can't it?" she asked.

"So we simplify."

I saw her smile as she leaned into me. "Right," she said, her voice hesitant. "We simplify."

She was in my arms, but it was her reflection in the window, unclear and a little dim from the darkness behind, that was looking back at me. Its expression seemed hard, inflexible, like a person who could never really change.

"Things could work out," I said. "If we keep trying, they will."

She didn't answer. A charred log dropped through the grate in the fireplace; embers sparked as it fell, then faded away. "Let's just get past tonight," she finally answered.

"And after that?"

She turned and looked up at me, our eyes met, then she rotated back around and glanced at the fire. "Whatever was meant to be," she said, "will happen."

"Some *grand design*?" I almost said, but didn't. I just kissed her neck again and remained silent.

PAUL F. WOLF is a special-education teacher in Chicago, where he has taught cognitive-learning disabled, behaviorally disordered, and autistic children for twenty-five years. He has published short fiction in about forty literary journals throughout the United States, including *Other Voices, Souwester, Puerto del Sol, The Georgetown Review* and *StoryQuarterly.* His first novel was released in spring 2001.

DONALD L. ROSE AND MIKE TAYLOR

In Pursuit of Donkeys

Finding a Kingdom Undreamed of

THREE GREAT MONARCHS IN THE OLD TESTAMENT were Saul, David, and Solomon. The earliest was Saul. He was a shy and humble young man who came from the smallest of Israel's tribes. He didn't mind saying that his family was the least of the families in the tribe.

Thus, as he grew up he had no notion of a king's crown in his future. Not for a moment did he dream of finding a kingdom. He was not aware that the people of Israel had demanded that they should have a king like the nations around them. But one day the donkeys of Saul's father strayed and were lost. The father said to the son, "Arise. Go look for the donkeys." (This is all in the Bible's ninth chapter of the book of Samuel.)

Saul undertook the search. He went this way and that way seeking those elusive animals.

He and his servant went through a mountainous region, but they did not find them. They passed through the land of Shaalim, and they were not there. They traversed the land of the Benjamites, but they did not find them.

Eventually, they found themselves in a neighborhood where there was a seer, or man of God. The idea occurred to them that they might try visiting this man, for they said, "Perhaps he can show us the way we should go." The man of God was Samuel.

The story takes on new intrigue when we learn what God had spoken in Samuel's ear the day before Saul came, saying, "Tomorrow I will send you a man from the land of Benjamin, and you shall anoint him King."

Imagine Saul's sense of good fortune when he asked a man at the city gate "where is the seer's house?" and when the man answered, "I am the seer." Saul must have marveled when the seer said, "As for your donkeys that were lost three days ago, do not be anxious about them."

While Saul was still intent on the missing donkeys, God commanded Samuel to perform the royal anointing. And so Saul's journey in search of donkeys resulted in his acquiring a kingdom.

Emanuel Swedenborg comments on the pursuits that occur in the growth and development of children. "At first they learn very many things, including those that are childish—games and so on—not to make them wise but to prepare them to receive the useful things that lead to wisdom." (*Secrets of Heaven,* paragraph 3470.)

The games we learned as children, even the ones not labeled "educational," prepare us for more mature undertakings. An athletic coach encourages young players to win a game and to execute their parts in it. But beyond the games, there are goals of character development, the discovery of moral strength, and the spirit of team cooperation. Especially there is the need to prepare ourselves to be useful in the human community.

Beyond this worldly life with its pursuits, is there a heavenly destiny? According to Swedenborg the whole of earthly life is preparation for a new life.

Swedenborg says, "The fact is that a person is in this world so as to be introduced through services he renders here into the activities which are of heaven. One's life in this world is hardly a moment in comparison with life after death, for this is eternal. (*Secrets of Heaven,* paragraph 5006.)

In our daily lives we sometimes feel we are in a "rat race." Perhaps it could be called a "donkey chase." Let the serendipity stories remind us that these pursuits are not all there is to life. Perhaps life holds for us surprises yet to come, some of them trivial, and some grand beyond our dreams.

DONALD L. ROSE is a grandfather who edits a monthly journal of Swedenborg studies, *New-Church Life.* MIKE TAYLOR lives in San Francisco. His cartoons regularly appear in *Tricycle, Writers Chronicle,* and *Modern Haiku.*

JOHN R. BUTLER

Jennifer's Cove

Frank W. Benson. *Morning Sunlight.* Watercolor, 1927. Peabody Essex Museum, Salem, Massachusetts. Private Collection. Photograph by Mark Sexton.

Summer 1984

TULLY REPEATEDLY STABBED THE OLD WOODEN PADDLE into the calm water, pulling with young strength. Table Rock Lake's clear waters hissed at the canoe's bow with each stroke.

Teen anger consumed him. He was taking it out on the paddle.

Serve my old man right if this stupid paddle broke. Told him he should buy one of those new laminated bent-shaft jobs.

But the cedar had been carefully selected for clear and straight grain a half century ago, and the shaft bent imperceptibly to each stroke, just enough so that it wouldn't break.

And this clunky old canoe—weighs twice as much as that white water Kevlar rig back at camp. A wonder the canvas hasn't rotted right off. I know he could afford a new one, but no, he says they don't have character. Character!

In his blind anger he almost ran into a girl drifting on an air mattress.

"Hey," she yelled, "watch your way!"

Her voice did much more than startle him. Her brogue captured his attention. Tully skillfully brought the canoe to a stop.

"Sorry," he mumbled, "I wasn't looking."

Tully was looking now. His eyes, responding to the obvious youth of her voice, looked for the usual expanses of firm young flesh, barely covered by a string bikini, blonde hair short with tight curls.

But he was disappointed. A white one-piece bathing suit seemed to cover her from thighs to shoulders, and a white bathing cap hid her hair.

Jeez, where did she get that outfit? Catalog? Thrift shop?

Then he finally looked at her face, just to see if there was anything worth looking at. *Freckles, wouldn't you know!*

*He was drawn to her eyes, greener than the old cano*e. They sparkled like sunlight on a rippled pond. The sudden leap in his heart, the catch in his breath: They caught him unaware.

For he saw admiration, even love in those eyes, a new sensation that left his head spinning.

Teen macho was about to take over when he realized her eyes were admiring the canoe!

"Old Town Guide model, isn't it? And the paddle—a genuine old beaver tail. Yours?"

Speechless for a moment, then: "No, not really. Its like, you know, my old man's." He started to add that he was saving up for a new Mad River canoe, but a rare flash of caution silenced him.

Tully noted that she still hadn't really looked at him, just at the old-fashioned canoe and paddle. That pinched his pride, even if she did look like something out of his mother's photo album. Why didn't those flashing green eyes look at him? He felt challenged.

"You handle it quite nicely," she said rather matter-of-factly, paused a very long moment, then finally looked Tully square in the eyes, "when you look where you are going."

Tully could feel his face flushing. "I'm sorry. Really. I was, like, . . . my mind was wandering."

"You were mad at someone and taking it out on that lovely old canoe. I could tell. But apology accepted. My name is Colleen. Yours?"

"Tully. And thanks." His mind was racing, trying to catalog the trill in her soft, low voice. "Irish?"

Colleen smiled a "yes," a marvelous smile that warmed Tully without making his face flush again.

"Tully is a fine old Irish name," she said. "Did you know? It means 'To live with the peace of God.'"

Disappointed by no reaction, she continued. "I love your old canoe. Would you mind if I paddled it someday?"

The stern voice of Tully's father surged through his mind: *"Mind you, no one—I repeat, no one—is to use this old classic except you. Understand? I'm not even sure I should let you use it."* They had traded bitter words about values, maturity, responsibilities. Tully had paddled off in a rage.

Now he saw Colleen's green eyes gazing at him, eyes filled with admiration, but not for him. "Sure. Want to go now? I'll paddle up to shallow water so you can get in."

"Not necessary. Just hold yourself steady."

So quickly that Tully barely realized what happened, Colleen boarded the canoe from deep water. He'd seen the instructor at camp demonstrate that technique, but none in his class had been able to perfect it, always swamping the canoe in the try.

Colleen retrieved her float and tossed it into the canoe. Her eyes took in the flawless varnish on the cedar planks and oak ribs, the thwarts and woven cane seats. "She is a beauty. Real character."

The trilled "r's" ran a ripple down Tully's back. Suddenly he liked "character." He also liked the way she called the canoe "she," not "it" like his father did.

"Yeah, she's an Old Town Guide model," answering her first question, ignored up to now, "over fifty years old. Paddles, too. What'd you call 'em?"

"Beaver tails. Think about it." She picked up the second paddle, balanced it with satisfaction in her left hand, then began paddling with obvious ease.

With her penetrating green eyes no longer able to watch him, Tully stared at the curves of Colleen's back, mentally stripping her of the all-covering white suit, down to the usual string bikini—or less.

Then, as she commenced paddling, he noted—his teen values were shocked to discover—that the white suit did more than cover her back. The strong, smooth flow of her back from shoulders to hips was emphasized, not hidden. The muscles in her back, in continual interplay with each stroke, wove a sensuous beauty wholly new to him.

"My grandfather had an Old Town, much like yours." Colleen's voice came easily, her strong yet seemingly effortless strokes not robbing her breath.

"I spent many holidays with him," she continued, "he taught me all I know about canoeing."

Tully didn't know whether to admire her grandfather, or to be mad at him for producing a student more skilled than himself.

Then, with only a brief pause in her steady stroke, she pulled off the white swim cap.

"Jesus," Tully gasped under his breath as waves of Irish-red hair fell down over her shoulders, reaching for the small of her back.

"Did He answer?" she asked.

"Huh?"

"You called out to our Lord. He always answers me. I just wondered if he answered you, too?"

Momentarily lost for words, Tully's mind raced. What's with this chick? Then, admiring the flaming long tresses and the way they enhanced without fully covering her back, he smirked and muttered "Yeah, He sure did."

Ignoring the implications of his reply, Colleen returned to her train of thought. "Grandfather loved that canoe so much. At his wake it was given to me with much ceremony." A long pause. "Now he will always be with me."

Another long pause, and Tully saw a break in her smooth rhythm as her hand went to her face. She's wiping away a tear? Oh, give me a break!

"He was a wise man, and his greatest legacy to me was more than a classic canoe, it was his love of God, of beauty, and the ability to appreciate beauty in all forms. Yes," she said, now more to herself, "he will always be with me."

Tully had seen her shoulders sag perceptibly as she spoke of the wake, then brace for even more-perfect strokes, as if her grandfather had whispered to her in a heavy brogue. Unaccustomed to death, or to expressing sympathy, he mumbled, "Sorry 'bout him."

Then they paddled in silence for some minutes, Colleen absorbed in thoughts of her grandfather. Tully pondered the realization that he could admire a stunning young woman—even girl seemed somehow inappropriate—without the usual teen fantasies of groping sex.

"Tully," Colleen started hesitantly, "Please call me Jennifer. That is my middle name, and grandfather preferred it, always called me that. He said it sounded . . . safer."

Tully's mind questioned the odd emphasis, and she continued. "And it just seems more comfortable to me when I'm canoeing."

"Sure, Jennifer." Then he added some comment with a vulgar word in it. No big deal, just the most common four-letter word all his friends used. Jennifer stopped paddling, turned in her seat and looked Tully square in the eyes. "Please!" was all she said, but her eyes said so much more.

Steeped in a culture which encouraged violent action or vulgar language, Tully was surprised that he could even read her eyes. The hurt he saw knifed into him. Even worse, he sensed that the welling tears were not because she had been offended, but that her budding admiration for him had been crushed.

"Uh, I'm sorry. Y'know?" Tully really didn't know how to apologize, but then he made a silent and surprising vow to himself. As if she sensed the import of his awkwardness, Colleen put the matter behind her. And Tully never cursed again. Never.

"Where are we going?" she asked.

"To the end of this cove. Used to be Mill Creek, before the dam flooded it. Now we call it Mill Creek Cove. The end isn't far, y'know."

"Interesting. And no, I didn't know," she replied, but the retort went over Tully's head. "Are you still in school?"

"Yeah, senior in Green Forest, just south of here."

"I'm a senior too, in Belfast. Do you camp here often?"

"Every summer at the Mill Creek Campground. Your first summer here? I don't remember you." He paused, added an afterthought: "I would have remembered you."

Jennifer was glad she wasn't facing Tully, showing her blush. "Yes, my first. My aunt—she's a professor at the College of the Ozarks—asked me to holiday with her. I think she thought it might help me get over the loss of my grandfather. She . . ." Jennifer lapsed into silence, then more openly wiped away tears.

They paddled in silence for long minutes, their strokes slower and easier, not wanting to reach the cove's end too soon, not wanting to break a developing spell.

Tully finally broke the silence. "I've got a problem."

"Oh?"

"I promised my old man I wouldn't let anyone else use his canoe. It's sort of his baby."

"And now you don't know what to say to him. Or if you should. You broke your word."

"Yeah."

Jennifer wished he would say "yes." "Yeah" sounded so inarticulate. *I'll work on that, too,* she thought, then let it pass. "Well, honesty *is* the best policy, after all. You could say I haven't really used his canoe, that I'm just your guest in it. You were simply showing proper hospitality to a first-time visitor to your fair country."

A long pause while Tully mulled the conversation with his father. "I think you're right." Another pause. "I *know* you are. Want to go paddling again tomorrow?"

"In the afternoon, sure. We're going to church in the morning. Do you attend?"

"Sometimes Mom does." A long pause. "My old man doesn't believe."

"You mean your father? What a tragedy."

"I guess I'd never thought about it." Then he did think about it. "Maybe so."

Mostly perfect summer days found Jennifer and Tully paddling the Old Town ever increasing distances from the Mill Creek campground, exploring lovely and remote coves from south of Logslide Bluff to west of Philibert Bluff, but always returning to that most beautiful cove of them all, up Mill Creek.

"This is quite my favorite cove, Tully. When we paddle past that last bend, it seems like we are in another world, all of our cares left far behind. It seems so safe and snug here. Now that I can trust you."

Tully winced. Just once had he tried to make an intimate advance. It was expected behavior in his culture, but Jennifer's withering look of shock, her silent disapproval, stirred a latent sense of decency.

The shoreline of gray weathered rocks, hardy native willows, olive-green young sycamores and blue-green cedars provided the serene backdrop to occasional visits by deer, mink, fox, and beaver.

Some days, after a picnic supper in the canoe, they waited for the sunset, then for dusk to deepen. First came the flights of bats. After they left, the whippoorwills and bullfrogs would start their choruses.

Occasionally Jennifer brought tapes of her playing her Irish harp, and Tully was entranced with the many songs she sang in accompaniment. He recognized only *Danny Boy,* but loved the traditional airs, and even tried to learn some of the Gaelic words so he could sing along.

Young love tried to blossom, but each was aware that at the end of two short weeks the vastness of the Atlantic Ocean would separate them.

So, instead, the old canoe became their bond of friendship, a common love to share, a safer love to cherish. It was their magic boat, their dream ship that took them to new and beautiful shores and coves, to intimacies of the mind.

But always they returned to the Mill Creek cove.

As their two-week vacations approached an end, Tully felt inspired, in a manner most uncharacteristic for callow teenagers, to commemorate their favorite cove. He had long called it "Jennifer's Cove" in his mind. Now he was moved to share the name.

"When I get back home, I'm going to make a sign that says *Jennifer's Cove,* and nail it to that tree right there." And he pointed his old paddle to a cedar close to the shore.

Jennifer was quiet and thoughtful for several minutes. "That would be quite perfect, Tully, but I have a request. Please make the sign read *Jennifer's Cove 1984.* I want this summer of 1984 to be remembered forever."

The inevitable goodbyes came, and were tearful. Jennifer surprised everyone, herself included, when she gently and briefly kissed Tully, their first kiss.

Her parting words to Tully were also brief: "Please look up Matthew 28.20."

Winter 1984–1985

NEVER BEFORE A LETTER WRITER, Tully found himself eagerly answering Jennifer's letters from Belfast. They wrote about canoes, folk music, nature, wildlife, and of course, Jennifer's Cove. But Jennifer avoided any mention of the continuing terrorism in Northern Ireland.

And over his desk was his carefully lettered little sign: "I am with you always. Mt.28.20"

At school, Tully found his circle of friends changing as newfound values and sense of decency alienated him from his old crowd.

Tully's father was puzzled but pleased with the new maturity, better friends, and a new interest in world affairs, most particularly about contemporary religion and civil unrest.

Then one day the mail brought a rather bulky envelope addressed in an unfamiliar hand from Belfast. His father took it to Tully and discreetly withdrew.

Later, hearing muffled sobbing from Tully's room, he knocked on the door, then entered. "What is it, son?"

Unable to speak, Tully handed him the envelope. Enclosed was his last letter to Jennifer, unopened, a newspaper clipping, and a note from her family. Jennifer had been one of the first of the dozens that would die in 1985, a victim of a random act of terrorism, killed on her way home from school.

Living amidst violence, she had apparently worried about the possibility, and had told her father that if anything ever happened to her, she wanted her grandfather's treasured Old Town canoe to be sent to Tully. Her father wrote that he was complying.

Months later a delivery truck brought the long crate to Tully's home, and he opened it with tears in his eyes. Like his father's canoe, it was green, the color of Jennifer's eyes. And near the stern seat, applied in small gold leaf, was *"I am with you always."*

Summer 1996

HELPED BY HIS WIFE SUE, Tully carefully lifted the old green canoe from the station wagon and set it at the shoreline, down from their tent at the Mill Creek campground.

Off for summer break from his teaching position at the College of the Ozarks, Tully thought it was finally time for his family, and the old canoe, to paddle south into Jennifer's Cove.

"Mommy," asked the older child, "tell me again the story about *The Enchanted Cove.* Please?"

Sue paused paddling and looked back at Tully. He smiled and nodded.

"A long, long time ago, there was an angry young man. He didn't know why he was angry, it just seemed cool. Well, he met this princess from a far land. In a magic boat they often went to the enchanted cove. Now the princess knew that the angry young man was really a good person, just pretending to be bad. So she worked very hard to bring out the good, and to get rid of the bad.

"She also worked very fast, for she had only two weeks to change him. But for such a young princess, she was very wise and used things he knew well to teach him about things that were new to him. And she used her great beauty to teach him that beauty is a gift to be given, not taken."

"Did she change him, Mommy, did she?" asked the older child.

"Yes, dear, she really did change him."

"How do you know that she changed him?"

"I knew him when he was angry. He was good looking, but he wasn't nice. But after many visits to The Enchanted Cove, he became very nice, too."

"What was the magic boat like, Mommy?"

"It was a canoe, and it looked just like this one." Anticipating the next question, Sue continued. "And we are paddling into The Enchanted Cove, just as they did."

Now the oft-repeated bedtime story ventured into new waters. Sue asked: "Do you know who the angry young man was?" The children shook their heads "no," and she continued. "Look behind you. You will see him in the back of *our* magic boat."

They looked back, around and past their daddy, then looked at him. He smiled and nodded his head, "Yes, I was the angry young man." Anticipating their next question, he continued. "I never saw that beautiful princess again. She went back to her faraway land, then God called her to try to find the good in many other angry people."

"What was the princess' name, Mommy?" asked the older child.

"Colleen Jennifer."

The two small girls looked at each other and giggled. "That's our names!" they said as one.

"Yes," said Sue, "if Princess Colleen Jennifer hadn't changed your daddy, you wouldn't be here today."

The girls looked at each other, not really understanding.

Tully paddled close, then waded ashore, carrying a large bag from the canoe.

Colleen, Jennifer, and Sue watched as he pulled an old piece of plywood, squirrel-chewed at the edges, letters fading, from a cedar close to the water's edge.

In its place he fastened a more permanent sign made of old barn oak, weathered as gray as the rocks, with letters and numbers deeply engraved into the wood. The inscription read: *Jennifer's Cove, 1984.*

"And now you know, girls, that our Enchanted Cove is really named Jennifer's Cove. Now we can always come back here, read the sign, and know how a young princess named Jennifer taught this angry young man to be good enough to become your father."

JOHN R. BUTLER, a professional writer, was formerly a Coast Guard Search and Rescue pilot, flying amphibians and helicopters, retiring as a Commander in 1974. Unable to find the true story of the real *Jennifer's Cove* sign, he wove this story from his faith, love of canoes, and the actual setting.

CHARLES M. WHITE

The Eye of the Storm

John Orne Johnson Frost. *Sable Island: The Sailor's Graveyard.* Water-based paint and pencil on wallboard, 1922–1928. Abby Aldrich Rockefeller Folk Art Museum, Colonial Williamsburg Foundation, Williamsburg, Virginia.

The following records, and statements are available to corroborate this account.

- *Naval logs of the* U.S.S. Park County *(LST-1077) are in the possession of the United States Navy Department in Washington, D.C.*
- *A witness to the events pertaining to the storm and what transpired after the storm can be contacted through the customer service department for Trans World Airlines in Norfolk, Virginia. Her name is Margaret Clark.*
- *The author of this account was a fireman (E-3) stationed aboard the* U.S.S. Park County *during this time frame. His name can be found on the Duty Roster, also in the possession of the U.S. Navy Department in Washington, D.C.*

IT WAS IN THE FALL OF SEVENTY-ONE, late in the season for the rains had come, and the monsoons were upon us—a time of hurricanes, tornadoes, and typhoons. We had just been relieved off the line in Vietnam after hauling bullets, bombs, and beer to the boys in the bush up along the Mei-Kong, all the way to Cambodia. Ninety days on the line without a break. A year and a half in that war-torn hell without once setting my feet on American soil; we were all due a break.

We were about four hours out of Cameron Bay when the old man's voice came across the PA system, telling the crew of the orders we had just received from COMNAV Seventh Fleet. We were bound for glory, a three-day stop in Subic Bay in the Philippine Islands to take on fresh supplies, then ten days across the big blue waters to Pearl Harbor in the Hawaiian Islands, where we would take on stores and supplies destined for our next port-of-call, the island of Guam, some fifty-three hundred miles across open waters.

Now for you landlubbers, this was not a place to go—just a big old desolate rock stuck out in the middle of the ocean, inhabited by gooney birds and a handful of sailors who had the misfortune to end up stationed there. From there, we would again put out to sea; our next port-of-call was the enchanting land down under. From that port, we would sail for home just beyond the Golden Gate and a long, sought-after and well-deserved leave.

Little did we know that the best made plans of the Seventh Fleet would turn to dust and take their place, like so many others before them, at the bottom of Davy Jones' locker, lost forever beneath the deep blue waters. The land of enchantment and wonder would not be ours to claim on this trip, and this crossing would be like no other we had ever made before—for the Lord in all His power and wisdom had need of the *USS Park County* (LST-1077) and its crew for one more mission, perhaps the most important mission of her career.

Now before I tell the events of this crossing, let me first tell you about the *Park County.* She had seen many tours and many years of faithful service to the USA, and this was to be her last trip. She was going home to be retired from active service, and she was going home in honor and dignity, for she had earned the right.

The old gal was not a big ship. She had a crew of just over a hundred men, not like those huge floating bird farms, which you landlubbers call an aircraft carrier. The *Park County* was small, only a mere three hundred and eighty-two feet long and a paltry fifty feet wide. Her well deck (cargo space) was barely over fourteen feet in depth. She was outfitted with three-inch guns, one mounted fore and aft and two amidships, one to port and one to starboard. Though not heavily armed, she was a scrapper and would stand to the last man against any act of aggression that was brought against her.

You see, it was the heart of the crew that made this floating arsenal, with her cargo of death and destruction—a formidable adversary in any man's eyes. She was slow in the water; her top speed even when she was empty was a scant fourteen knots, and when she was loaded, she would top out at barely eleven. That's to say, she would cover about eleven nautical miles in one hour, and we were setting out on an ocean voyage that would cover nearly fourteen thousand miles. Yes, sir, it would be a long time before we would reach the Golden Gate and home.

The trip from Cameron Bay to the Philippine Islands was the short leg of the journey. Three days out, we sighted the entrance to the naval installation at Subic Bay in the Republic of the Philippines; then we spent three days in port to off-load the supplies and take on new stores and make ready to get underway. On the morning of the fourth day, we cast off all lines and put out to sea. Our next port of call was some fifty-three hundred miles away, nearly one-fifth of the way around the world, if running at flank speed and blessed with prevailing winds.

If we were lucky at all, we should reach Pearl Harbor in about twenty days. The crossing was like a vacation in itself; warm sun-filled days and the balmy breezes of the western winds at our backs carried us peacefully across the ocean. On the morning of the tenth of August, we entered the port of the naval installation at Pearl Harbor in the Hawaiian Islands. The second leg of our journey was complete without event in this four-legged deployment. The next three days were filled with sand, sun, work, and fun as we prepared for the next segment of our cruise.

On the morning of the thirteenth of August, we cast off all lines and made ready to get underway. Less than an hour out to sea, the order came down from the comm to batten down the hatches, secure all gear, and prepare for rough weather. We saw the storm before it overtook us, for there she blew, coming up on our fantail at a high rate of speed which we could not outrun. The sight that we beheld put fear in our hearts. There behind us, not more than a half-mile beyond the ship's wake, was a tube of water of massive size. It reached from the ocean's surface to over ninety feet straight up toward the heavens. There was fear in the men's hearts at this awesome sight, this funnel of awesome power and impending doom. So strong was the scent of fear aboard that tiny ship that you could cut it with a knife. There was no time to turn and run and no place to run, for all around us was nothing but open sea as far as the eye could see, and we were like a twig floating on a lake.

It was in that moment that I came to understand the meaning of the word faith, for I knew in my heart of hearts that the only thing that could save us now was the hand of God. Nothing else could stay the power and ferocity of the storm that was bearing down upon us. As I continued to pray to God to save us from Mother Nature's rage and fury, a strange peace came over me, and I knew in an instant that we were going to be all right.

As we all stood in silence watching the storm overtake us, a miracle was in the making. In the time it takes to blink your eye, the storm lifted off the ocean surface as though a hand from above us had just plucked it from our path. However, this was not meant to be, for in the next second the storm settled back upon the ocean's surface. Instead of being on the outside and running from it, we were now caught in its eye and being carried within the storm itself!

At this time, the order came down from the bridge for all off-duty personnel to lash themselves into their bunks and not to leave them except for necessary reasons, such as eating and performing their assigned duties.

Being an impressionable young man in my early twenties, and not being prone to following orders to the letter, natural curiosity overcame my fear. I had to see what was about, so I thought one little peek would not cause any problem. With this thought in mind, I made my way to the mess deck located amidships and on the same level as the main deck of the ship. As I undogged the hatch and stepped out onto the main deck, a feeling of awe overtook me as the hatch slammed shut behind me. For, there before me and all around the ship, I could see nothing but water from the ocean floor spiraling upward to over forty feet above the highest point on the ship.

Far above me at the top of the tube was a bright light illuminating this giant wall of water. A great wind could be heard all around us, though there was not a movement of air within the tube of water where we were riding. I had seen enough. I knew at that moment we were truly in the Lord's hands, and only he could bring us through this storm safely. I quietly reentered the ship and left God to do His work as I returned to the engine room to do mine.

Shortly after I returned to the engine room, the order came down from the helm to reduce the engine's speed to a standby position (which in layman's terms is like neutral in an automobile). It was brought to our attention that the storm was carrying us at a speed twice that which we could attain under our own power.

Time moved on as we were swiftly transported across the ocean, held in the bosom of the storm, and protected from its force only by a higher power. For seven days and seven nights we rode in the belly of the storm; not once did the gale force winds rock the ship; not once did the wall of water swirling around us come down upon us. We were sort of like Jonah in the belly of the whale.

In the early morning hours of the eighth day, the storm left us —gone in the night—and the sea we now rode upon was peaceful and tranquil. The ocean surface was like a sheet of glass broken only by the cutting action of the bow of the ship as she forged ahead and the gentle wake that fell off behind us.

As I stepped out on the main deck that morning to enjoy my first cup of coffee and a smoke and to give thanks to the Lord for sparing our lives, I was brought to an awareness that truly amazed me. There before us, not more than a half-mile away was the entry to an island port. I knew that port from times past. I had been there often before; it was the entry to the port at Aganna, Guam. Then, I realized the awesome power and the miraculous crossing we had made. The storm had brought us across thirty-eight hundred miles of ocean to deposit us at the doorway of our destination in less than half the time that it would have taken us under our own power.

As I stood there with my fellow shipmates enjoying my morning coffee and the feeling of peace that now overtook us, suddenly all hell broke loose as the shipboard alarms went off sending all hands to battle stations. I stood there wondering why, after all we had just come through, would we be going through general quarter drills in U.S. waters. I truly felt the old man had slipped a cog, you know, gone round the bend so to speak.

Well, I'm here to tell you that thought lasted about as long as it took me to think it, for there before my very eyes came a giant warship from out of the murky depths. She was so close to us that I probably could have thrown my cup and hit her.

As she broke the surface, all my questions were answered in the blink of an eye. The ship before us bore the distinct markings of the Russian Navy, and she had no business in that part of the world, let alone in U.S. territorial waters. The old man gave the order, and all starboard guns were brought to bear. A warning shot was put across the bow of the Russian sub, and in an instant she was gone from our sight.

To this day I believe the hand of God had moved us across the ocean to that particular place and at that specific time to stave off an open act of aggression.

After his tour of duty in the U.S. Navy, CHARLES M. WHITE became a cross-country trucker throughout a thirty-year career. Many situations came into his life that bore the trademark of God's hand. These testimonies can be found in a book entitled *The Ever Present Hand,* to be published in 2003.

JOHN PASCAL

Consider the Lilies . . .

Paul Strand. *Chair Abstract, Twin Lakes, Connecticut. 1916.* ©1985 Aperture Foundation Inc., Paul Strand Archive.

I WAS REPAIRING THE PEDIMENT OF A LALLY COLUMN IN THE CELLAR with some stone mix I got from my dentist when I last went to him for a free checkup (and reminding myself that when I took the cat in for *her* annual checkup, I must remember to ask the vet about the pain I've been having in my left side) when the phone rang. Cursing the interruption, I put down the old but good trowel I'd collected along with my father's other tools from the family house after he'd died and my mother had moved into a smaller place, and went upstairs to the phone. It must have rung ten times before I got there.

I liked this phone, the one I'd disconnected from my desk and taken with me when I'd retired from the Army. It was black and heavy and had a dial with big numbers, nothing like those little light plastic ones so easy to knock off the table, those with the little buttons that my big klutzy fingers would often push two at a time. Anyway, when I said "Hello," the voice at the other end asked if I were so and so, and I responded that I might be if he told me what he wanted. He said he'd seen among newly copyrighted manuscripts at the Library of Congress one by me (if I was who he thought I was), that he thought it was a great novel and wondered if I would be interested in "subsidy publication." The word "publication" came through loud and clear, but the adjective which preceded it was muttered, almost unintelligible. It sounded like Sun City, as in perhaps Sun City Publications, which might have meant, to the uninitiated, that some new publishing house in Miami or Phoenix was interested in getting me into print the old fashioned way, with *their* money. "How are you spelling that word just before 'publication'?" I asked politely. When he got to the third letter, I slammed the phone down.

Cursing pretty freely now, I went back to my work in the cellar, only to discover before much time had passed that I needed a little more stone or cement patch, whatever the hell it's called. That damned dentist—you'd think that as long as he was parting with some of his precious product, he could have given me a decent amount! Now, cursing the dentist as well as the recent caller (and finally, the cat, who had just tested my patch work for firmness with an inquisitive paw), I left the house for the Adirondack village hardware store five miles away.

As I drove along the snowy road in the twenty-year-old Mazda I'd bought for $1,000 cash—which, because of its age and lack of electronic sophistication, I was still able to maintain and repair myself (except for truly major work, anyway)—I reflected upon that novel about which that slick telephone pest had spoken. Hard to be objective, I know, but still . . . .

There are times when, having reread and then read again those books I treasure in my library (of more than two-thousand volumes, almost exclusively used books), I resort to something which I have written—a short story, a novel, a poem, a prudential nonfiction work based upon the experiences I've had, some good, some bad, others verging on the paradisiacal or horrible—after leaving my teaching post mainly due to the pressures and strictures of "political correctness." Now I found myself nodding agreeably that that latest novel, barring any glaring "plot holes" or other howlers was, certainly by today's careless standards, a damned good read. As I drove into the village, I found myself wishing I could afford to pay some sort of intelligent, honest critic to provide a second and more honestly objective opinion.

Having parked the car and retrieved nine pennies someone had discarded recently enough so that they'd not been trodden into the snow, I began to cross the street to the hardware store. As I waited for a speeding truck loaded with lumber to pass, a twenty-foot molding strip that obviously hadn't been properly secured went flying into the street, landing intact and more or less in the right lane. Oblivious to his loss, the truck driver continued on his way. With one large gloved hand, I held up approaching vehicles, and with the other hand I quickly retrieved the willowy length of molding. I grimaced regretfully as I broke the thing nearly in half, but it was the only way to store it in my little car (even then with a pair of four-foot ends sticking out of the front passenger window).

After rolling the window snugly up against my protruding newly-acquired possession(s) and seeing nothing else that warranted my attention, I crossed the street and went into the store. Barring one smiling fat woman with a baby carriage outside the store, no one seemed to have taken any notice of my little foray. Of course, once inside the store, the first question I had for the shopkeeper was how much a linear foot of one-inch, quarter-round yellow pine molding might cost me.

On my way home I laughed in spite of myself. And then I remembered Guy De Maupassant's *A Piece of String,* a story I'd read for the first time in grammar school. You know the one: where a harmless and very conservative man (much as I see myself) while walking down his village street sees a piece of string, picks it up, and puts it in his pocket for possible future use. At about the same time, a wealthy resident of the same village loses his wallet. Someone, having seen the man pick up something in the street, reports this to the police who, in their investigation of the missing wallet, turn quite naturally upon the innocent man. *Au fond,* the truth is revealed, but although the poor man's freedom is restored, his reputation is not; at best he is put down as a stingy old eccentric.

Though knowing myself as being closely similar to this poor character, I can't say I've really worried that something akin to such a predicament might befall me (as to the molding strip, there is always that fat woman who witnessed my little find); I suppose I will forever look for more-or-less honest ways to save a little money. Perhaps my childhood in the Bronx during the Great Depression has had something to do with this proclivity toward miserliness—once, while walking down White Plains Road with my mother, I found a nickel on the sidewalk, retrieved it, and gave it to her. Hell, in those days for a nickel you could ride the subway from 242nd Street all the way to Coney Island! (As a reward), I got a Batman comic book, which today might be worth a couple hundred dollars.) Now, on those rare occasions when I do visit a service garage, I almost always find a nut, or a bolt, or a cotter pin, or some other useful discarded object. Well, I've never had money, not real money, and, if I had, I probably wouldn't change; I'd still be walking around with my eyes on the ground.

When I arrived at the house, I checked my answering machine for messages. Oho! you'll say, what's a man with a phone such as the one he's just described doing with an answering machine? Well, you'd be right, except that I live alone, have submitted a number of my manuscripts (all written in pencil on long yellow legal pads, then typed on a second-hand Royal portable) for publication (all rejected), and, although that smart-assed cat can knock a ringing phone off the hook, she can't take a message.

There was one call on the machine from a youthful-sounding producer on the West Coast who had just finished reading my first novel—no, not the one that other guy was calling about, but one I'd submitted to any number of publishing houses who had rejected it the same number of times. I called him back immediately. Yes, he was "crazy about the book," and he offered me a quarter of a million dollars for the rights to adapt it for the screen! And, yes, he said, I could have first crack at doing the screenplay; and, of *course*, I could bring the cat with me to Hollywood! He seemed willing to talk endlessly, to the point where I felt I had to say I was "glad that it's your nickel, not mine," at which he paused, and asked me how old I was. So of course I lied ambiguously and Jesuitically and said I'd never see forty again. However true, this avoided his specific question (by more than a quarter-century) and seemed to reassure him.

NOW, AS I SIT ON THE VERANDAH of my beachfront house in Malibu watching the calm blue Pacific rolling into my sugary strip of beach, I find myself wondering what I did with that twenty feet of new quarter-round molding. Damn! I left it in the cabin I sold (at a profit) back East.

But wait. What's that down on the beach? A broken chair? Well, heck, there's no one around, and it's on my property, more or less. . . .

JOHN PASCAL's published books include *The Dartist,* a novel of intrigue, *Antipodes 10,* and its successor *Antipodes 20,* two books of short stories. He has won a *Writer's Digest* first prize for poetry and a short-story prize in London's *The European.* He lives in the foothills of the Adirondacks where he continues to write prose and poetry.

LEE BRAMBLE

The Messengers

What messages, one from the gods, one from man,
what messages bring these messengers to us?

Sultry, the legionnaires still at their posts,
the sea air mixing with the sweet smell of sweat,
of dung and leather and grapes along the walls—
bathers by the shore, the water warm,
translucent, in the lazy August sun.
Then the air rises like the dome of a circus tent
billowing in the wind, sucking up all below
before it settles again. Without warning
the sky darkens, the ash and pumice fall
in sheets along the narrow, rutted streets,
molding man and beast and man-made shelters,
even loaves of bread. Covered eighteen
centuries—then, uncovered to the air,
a molded shape, a man, fallen, running
perhaps, running for his life, himself a message.

In the early morning sun, he races his bike,
intent, yellow telegram in hand,
watching his shadow as he pedals, the spokes spinning
in his mind, humming to his laughter as he rides along
the thronged ways. He does not hear the other
hum, high in the August sky, nor the sudden
plosion, the fierce fire-storm, the great, hot
wind which catches him from behind and leaves,
there on the pavement, his image in burnt ash,
the museum photograph his cenotaph.

LEE BRAMBLE is a retired academic living on a 1780 New England farm on which his wife, and later their children, grew up. He has lived in China, England, Germany, and Austria, and traveled in Europe, Asia, and South Asia.

PART V

Being Open and Alert

mayflowers
candle-like green flames
now light up
the dark-leafed woods floor
their warm spring vigil
—Art Stein

The simplest and most powerful
method for personal spiritual development
in Swedenborg's theology
lies in the idea of usefulness . . .
Part of its beauty is its simplicity,
which permits carrying it out
in the midst of ordinary duties and labor,
indeed, in any human act.
It can be applied anywhere, anytime, by anyone.
Part of its power lies in its wonderful concreteness.
Much of religion
has to do with masses of words and ideas.
Usefulness *lies in concrete acts.*
Words are unnecessary.
The very concrete immediacy of useful action
takes us out of ourselves,
out into circumstances,
out toward others and a larger world.
—Wilson Van Dusen
Usefulness

RAE HALLSTROM

Floating into Tomorrow

Like two dozen party favors at a giant's birthday bash
Hot air balloons rise each year over Ravenna
Buoyed on the sweet succor of September winds
And memories of the town's
Toy balloon manufacturing plant.

Sometimes, the best we can do is stay afloat,
Never knowing exactly where the currents will carry us.
Below, even the big wheels are nothing but munchkins,
Waving, as if to the Wizard of Oz
And the lost chance for a free ride home
In Auntie Em's floating wicker basket.

All those slack-mouthed faces
Watching the dotted kaleidoscope of sky.
It's like reading tea leaves,
Phoning a psychic, or wishing on a star,
This sense of wanting to get on with life,
But first, seeking a map with step-by-step directions
And satisfaction guaranteed.

Despite the whimsical circus clown name,
The "Patches" balloon doesn't split at the seams.
And neither do we, when flight tested.
Once inflated, the balloons launch like so many
Cork-bottled messages,
Bobbing on the ocean of wind.

We are all of us adrift,
Babes in baskets of our own design.
Might as well enjoy the atmosphere,
While we gather courage for a change in course
At the Ravenna Balloon-A-Fair.

RAE HALLSTROM lives in Ohio with three teenagers, two cats, one dog (an Australian Shepherd), and Joe, her husband of twenty-two years. They are teaching her not to make promises she cannot keep. In her spare time she does the dishes and walks the dog. The dictionary is her favorite book because all the others are waiting to be discovered within it.

ANNE MCGINLEY

A Fool's Errand

Unknown artist.
St. Christopher.
Bronze, $8 \times 4^{5}/_{16} \times 2^{3}/_{8}$ in., Italian or Northern European, fifteenth century. ©2002 Museum of Fine Arts, Boston. Arthur Tracy Cabot Fund.

OLD BENAIAH'S SLEEVE WAS STILL DAMP when he got home. The sheep and goats had leaned their warm shoulders into his today, not budging from the water, when he'd reached between them for the rock. Now, before his eyes could adjust to the smoky darkness in his house, he felt in his bag for it. The stream had rolled the stone as perfectly round as the sun, and just small enough to fit his poor grandson's hand.

As soon as Benaiah's feet were clean he hurried to Abidon's mat on the floor. They would laugh together when he told him about the kid leaping onto the billy goat's back today. He knew the child would like to do that himself. Before the accident he would race with the goats, clambering over rocks; and he could coax them past the sheepfold's fragrant grain just by calling their names in his sweet voice. Benaiah smiled; he'd boasted about this many times to the neighbors, who of course struggled with their goats.

But at the bed he stopped. Abidon was sleeping again, black curls pressed to pale cheeks. Benaiah knelt and touched a lock with a roughened finger. The boy's skin had become so transparent, it seemed his spirit could slip right through it and disappear.

Benaiah let the rock roll silently to the floor. He went to Keturah who knelt by the oven.

"Where's his mother?" he asked.

"Getting water."

"The bandage is soaked through," he said. His wife sighed and nodded.

"He needs a new one."

"Yes." She didn't move. "He won't eat. He hardly drank anything all day."

"Did the midwife stop by?"

"She gave me more herbs, but I don't see them helping." She looked toward the boy. "We've tried everything."

Benaiah shut his eyes, started to speak, stopped. Finally he said, "Just change the bandage."

When she took clean rags to the bed, Benaiah stared down into the blazing length of the oven. Such a narrow hole in the floor it was, really; any man could step across it. But its clay walls stretched hot and deep into the ground.

Abidon cried out as she peeled the bandage off. His injury had seemed small at first. The boy had been running, and had tripped just here and fallen toward the oven. His mother had quickly seized his arm and snatched him out. Only his heel had swept in and burned against the hot clay.

Benaiah smelled from here the infection that had already eaten away the foot and was creeping toward Abidon's knee. He would never run with the flocks, never even walk again, anyone could see that. If they could just stop the infection. If only he would live.

Benaiah ducked out the door and fled to where the gnarled trees grew together. Then in his grief he wept, and cried out, "Blessed are you O God; all your ways are truth and your judgment is righteous." He wiped his face on his sleeve and whispered. "There's a sky full of sadness in me, God, because Abidon is dying. You know I have no other child to be my heir. Have mercy on me, O Lord. Command that he be restored to me so he and all our descendants may worship you."

HE RETURNED TO FIND A STRANGER waiting at his house. Hebrew travelers could expect hospitality from their brethren, so Benaiah welcomed him. Over dinner the man described a prophet and a crowd of followers he had seen. One woman, he said, lay almost too crippled to move.

"Her hands curled in like this." He showed him. "Anyway, this prophet says something to her and touches her head. Well, she sat up as straight as we're sitting here now, then—you should have seen her face. So . . . well, so happy to move . . . and then she just got up and walked around. Like she'd never had a problem at all. Except she was just shouting with happiness."

Keturah brought more wine in. Her face was blank as she filled the cup, as though she thought of nothing but the wine she poured.

"A modern prophet, really something to see," the man said, nodding, then glanced at the corner where Abidon lay. He leaned toward Benaiah. "I'm telling you, this one could heal anything. Deaf, sick, possessed, they all came away from him healthy and . . . and hearing, seeing, everything."

THAT NIGHT, while the visitor snored on his mat, Benaiah and Keturah whispered in bed.

"It must be the prophet Jesus we heard of before," she said, "and now he's so close. Didn't he say just two Sabbath days' journey, over by the sea?"

Benaiah shrugged in the dark. "Two Sabbath days by the main road. Longer our way."

"Still, so close."

"Keturah. I can't carry Abidon there. And none of the servants can take him. How could they haggle for . . . this?"

"Certainly, you're right." There was a silence.

"These stories—they can't be true. Many robes make a poor man fat."

"But what if they are true?" she asked. "It's the only hope we have."

The boy's mother whispered hoarsely from her bed. "If he is moved he will die all the sooner! Someone has to go and get the healer to come here to Abidon."

Silence again. Then Keturah said quietly, "Yes. Someone has to bring him here." A pause. "It's the only hope we have."

BENAIAH LEFT AFTER SUNRISE and walked narrow trails winding past hill after brown hill. In all his life he had never taken the main road, and these paths were as familiar as Keturah's face. He was a fool, he knew it, going off like this; and for what? He rubbed his neck, wondering again how much he should offer the prophet. Of course he mustn't start too low or the man would be insulted and never come. But how high could he go? A quarter of his flock after Abidon's fever had left him and the leg scabbed over?

The midday heat burned now, and he peered ahead for the shade trees. This time of day he should be resting there, but every year his steps were a little stiffer, a little slower. Now, Abidon—if Abidon were here, he would be in the trees already, and would laugh his funny snorting laugh when Benaiah finally sat down. That boy, with raven hair and sparkling, golden eyes like his father's. Old grief mingled with the thirst in his throat. A man should never have to bury his only son, he thought for the thousandth time. Or his only grandchild.

AT SUNSET HE CAME OVER THE LAST HILL. His vision wasn't good, but he could see the sea sparkling through air thick with dust, smoke, and noise. He sat on the grass, gripping his bag. Blankets, tents, and throngs of people covered the land beside the water.

Finally Benaiah descended into the thinnest part of the crowd and, holding his breath, stepped carefully between blankets and children and cooking fires. He bought some roast lamb, then sat on his bag and silently picked the hair from the meat. A girl stood nearby, watching him; half her face was misshapen, with one eye wet and unseeing and a boneless cavern below it. Benaiah averted his eyes, looked into the crowd. Then he saw how many there were, the ill and the lame, the blind, the oozing, the insane man led by a rope around his neck. A few, probably lepers, lingered beyond the edge.

He took the meat and his bag up a hillside, away from all of them. As it grew dark, and oil lamps flickered like stars below, he saw a dark mass—people—gathering by the sea. The healer must be there, but would not travel with Benaiah tonight. There was no need to ask him now. And Benaiah was too weary to ask. Too weary, even, to gather dung for a fire. He spread his blanket and slept.

WITH THE FIRST BIRDSONG Benaiah rose stiffly and followed a smell of fresh leaves and water. He passed a woman sleepily stirring her cooking fire. A girl, who skipped, laughing, around her, could be the twin of the one at the meat vendor's, only this one's face was perfect. That other child, ah, it was unfortunate.

Today he would speak to the prophet. He, a simple shepherd, must somehow be eloquent, more compelling than all of the suffering at hand. Benaiah stopped walking, turned and squinted back at the girl. Her robe was the same reddish-brown as the girl's yesterday. If this were she—his heart leapt—if she were cured, then Abidon could be restored. Not to walking, certainly, because his foot was gone; but to life. Benaiah chose his words, fit them together. *Without you, he will die—maybe tomorrow! You must come, rabbi. What may I offer you?*

He pushed through a thicket to a little stream.

Heal my grandson, please, rabbi. He is my only heir and he is dying. I will give whatever you ask. Only come with me now—you must come now . . .

He washed his face and hands and drank the cool water. He prayed there among birdsong and sweet-smelling leaves before eating some of Keturah's bread.

When the sun had risen he followed a path through spindly shrubs toward the beach, his heart fluttering like a fire in a desert wind. *Please, rabbi, heal my grandson Abidon. He is my only heir and without your help he will die. I give whatever you ask.*

Here his path intersected another. A group of men came down the other trail, hair dripping from the stream. *Heal my grandson Abidon, rabbi, please.* He waited for them to go by; some greeted him with nods as they passed, but one stopped and looked intently at Benaiah. The man smiled, as at an old friend, and stepped toward him. Benaiah looked more closely at him. No, they hadn't met . . . but his face held a look he had never seen before. As though he knew Benaiah well and loved him utterly. Worry fell away. *Rabbi.* The words he was practicing still drifted through his mind. *Please heal my grandson Abidon. Nothing can make him well but you.*

A breeze blew through the bushes, and Benaiah noticed that the leaves were glowing as though made of green fire. The rocks shone with light; everything, he saw, *was* light. The man was walking down the path now. Benaiah slowly followed.

People had surrounded the men ahead, calling to them. The light and aroma faded as Benaiah shook his head. This—this was Jesus, the one he sought! He must ask him! Anxiety rushed back as he tried to push through the crowd. No invalids here; these people were all strong and hearty, some even dancing.

"Rabbi! Please!" he called out. "You must come and . . ." an elbow caught him in the stomach, knocking his breath away. He bent over, only for a moment, but when he could breathe again the crowd was too deep, too massive, and too loud to reach through. They swept down the hill to the beach, singing and shouting; he stumbled along in the middle of it all, trying to find a way to the front.

The crowd stopped at the water's edge and Benaiah began to push through. Abidon could be worse now, he must hurry. But before he had gotten past ten men, the healer and some others boarded a fishing boat and pushed out to sea. People walked into the water, waving and calling to him; the oars thrust the boat out and then beyond them. By the time Benaiah reached the water and shouted, it was far from shore.

He stood there a long time after it was out of sight. The words, *please, rabbi, you must help my grandson,* buzzed around his mind like flies. The others gathered up blankets and bags and asses to go, but Benaiah stared out to sea until the sun went down. He spent the night alone, then rolled up his blanket and trudged home.

What would he tell Keturah and Abidon's mother? That he had been face to face with the prophet and never asked? Never spoke a word? How could he explain the light, the fragrance, the look in the man's eyes? Of course he could have healed Abidon. He must have been an angel of God with eyes like that. And he, Benaiah, had not uttered one word to ask. He could not bear to face his family, could not bear to watch Abidon die. Still he put one foot in front of the other and plodded steadily home.

At sunset he came within sight of his gate. Someone waited there, watching for him. Would run in, no doubt, with the news that he returned alone. No, the person came toward him. A dark-haired servant boy he didn't recognize . . . hair as dark as Abidon's. The boy ran like a hart, calling joyfully. Benaiah faltered, then looked sharply at the figure almost here now. Abidon! It was Abidon, *running!* And now in his arms, shouting, "Grandfather!"

Benaiah wept, holding the boy. Then, loudly praising God, he held Abidon by the shoulders and looked down, blinking away tears, to see both flawless, brown, bare feet.

ANNE MCGINLEY writes in Eugene, Oregon.

RICHARD PLEVIN

Wanna Go Again?

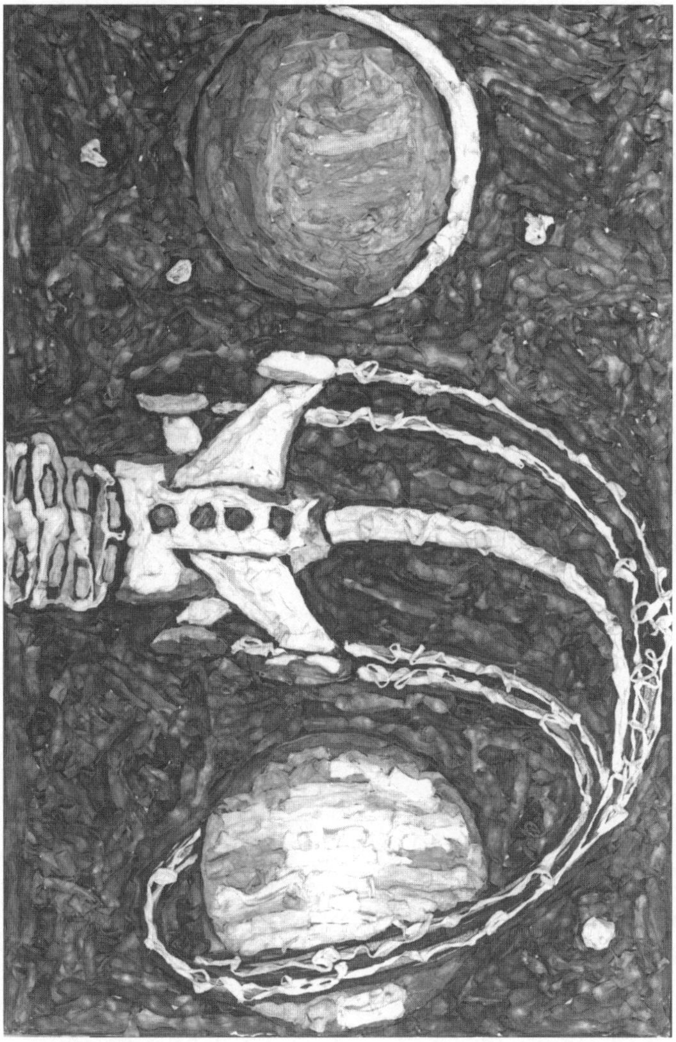

Joseph Zucker.
Otta Space.
Acrylic and rhoplex on canvas, 40×60 in., 1974.
Albright-Knox Art Gallery, Buffalo, New York.
Gift of Joel Shapiro, 1984.

IN 1979, WHILE ATTENDING COLLEGE IN ALBANY, my roommate Paul convinced me to jump out of a perfectly good airplane.

Paul was a natural athlete, and he was fearless. While most guys on the track team ran or jumped or threw pointy or weighty objects, Paul preferred to run full bore down a track, insert the tip of a twelve-foot Fiberglas pole into a small receptacle and launch his compact body ten feet into the air. He was the kind of guy who preferred to ski along the ridge of a sheer cliff, where a loss of control would result in certain death. Paul would hug the ridge, making effortless little turns, and still get to the bottom before the rest of us.

I had sufficient cause to suspect Paul's enthusiasm for skydiving. But some combination of rebelliousness and peer pressure—and the hope that it would improve my odds with women—convinced me to try it. So we signed up for the four-hour introductory training offered on campus that weekend by instructors from the skydiving club at Duanesburg airport, about twenty miles west of Albany.

The class was mostly technical information about "flying and landing" a parachute, including, appropriately, the inherent dangers involved. Although eight people attended the training, several bailed out after the first couple of hours. Of the remaining five, only three of us would actually jump the following weekend.

I was surprised to learn that parachutes don't drop straight down; they're designed to have a small forward velocity, say about five miles per hour—like a quick jog. To control direction, there are two small vents on the right and left, and two handles called toggles to open and close the vents. Open the right and air flows through faster, causing a lazy turn to the left. Open the left and turn right. Easy.

We also learned that for your first five jumps, they attach a "static line" to your rip cord so your chute releases automatically when you're about three yards from the plane. Your task as a beginning jumper is simply to fall out of an airplane from 4,000 feet. After the obligatory static line jumps, you graduate to free falling, meaning you're responsible for pulling your own rip cord. Assuming you survive that exercise, you progress through jumps from successively greater altitudes—from five, seven, nine and eleven thousand feet. When you jump from such heights, your body has time to reach "terminal velocity" and you stop accelerating as you plummet earthward. The friction of the air against your body increases with velocity—the faster you fall, the greater the friction. It turns out that it increases only until it matches the pull of gravity, at which point you experience weightlessness.

It sounded intriguing, but I did notice the word "terminal" echoing in my ears.

Falling at a constant speed is also one of the peculiarities of floating to earth with your parachute open. When you are just a few yards above ground, all the lessons acquired over a lifetime of jumping off stools, stairs, and chairs—without a parachute to slow you down—cause the newcomer to misjudge the moment of touchdown. To address that, we learned PLF—Parachute Landing Fall. Using PLF, you fix your eyes on the horizon as the earth approaches. Keeping your legs loose, you wait until you feel the first contact, then you crumple into a ball and execute a forward roll, absorbing the impact with your whole body. We practiced this by jumping off a five-foot platform to approximate the speed of impact.

When the instructor explained the possible modes of failure for the main parachute, I sat up a bit straighter. Sometimes the parachute remains spiked like a starched napkin, a condition you might correct by shaking the risers—thick straps connecting the harness to the many smaller suspension lines leading to the dome of fabric above. Other failures are more problematic, like the "partial inversion," caused by the inversion of one or more sections of the canopy, forming air pockets that give the nickname "Mae West" to this malfunction. This condition sometimes works itself out; sometimes the entire canopy turns inside out. Then there was the "streamer" or "cigarette roll," in which a bit of fabric blows between the suspension lines and rolls together with the opposite fabric. The friction of the rolling actually generates enough heat to fuse the nylon, leaving the canopy literally flapping in the breeze. In that case, you pull the cord on the emergency chute strapped across your belly and you pray.

The following Sunday, Paul and I borrowed a car and headed west to Duanesburg. Paul was energized. I was subdued, either from the previous night's cavorting or the growing recognition that I was committing a gross error of judgment. The butterflies in my stomach could have been due to either.

The puny airport looked more like a small town bus station: a minimal wooden building with no amenities beyond a water cooler, a bathroom, and a few cold wooden benches. There were two short, cracked runways and only a handful of propeller planes. Inside, we were greeted by a pleasant but slow-moving fellow about our age who seemed to wince when he moved his head too quickly. He directed us to the equipment racks, where we each selected a pair of tall lace-up boots, an insulated corduroy jumpsuit and a white crash helmet. My boots were too tight and my helmet too loose, but the overalls fit well enough.

It was a sunny but windy October day—windy enough to keep us grounded for several hours. We clomped around the office in our clumsy boots, alternating trips to the water cooler and the toilet.

Shortly after noon, they cleared our plane for takeoff. I climbed into my harness, snapping and adjusting until I was as comfortable as possible, given what felt like two seat belts riding high between my legs. The sturdy strap ran from crotch to shoulders and around my waist, holding the heavy main chute to my back and a smaller emergency shute across my belly. Clipped to the top of the emergency chute was a walkie-talkie in case the instructor needed to instruct us during our descent.

I looked at Paul, who now resembled some sort of covert military operative. This was partly owing to his attire, but mostly due to his swagger and the maniacal glint in his eyes. I swallowed hard against the lump in my throat and ambled out to the runway.

There were six of us jumping that day, three beginners, easily identified by our matching tan jumpsuits, and three seasoned skydivers with much flashier, happy-colored outfits and helmets. The experienced jumpers would be free-falling from a higher altitude after we beginners made our static line jumps. We were told that the plane would circle the airport and, accounting for the wind, drop us off so that we would float down to the football-field size plot abutting the runway. Then we would each gather up our chute, enjoy a few high-fives, and celebrate being alive.

The plane was a creaky two-propeller job with seats for the pilot and co-pilot and a hollow fuselage for the jumpers. After a seemingly slow-motion takeoff, we began our lumbering ascent to 4,000 feet. The instructor and the expert jumpers engaged the co-pilot in an animated chat about wind speed, atmospheric conditions, and the new parasail one of the jumpers was testing. Paul struck up a lively conversation with the other beginner, who had made his first jump the prior weekend and was still "totally stoked" by the experience. I listened and nodded, trying to seem at least slightly stoked.

When we reached our jump altitude, the instructor turned to the novices and asked who would be going first. Paul, ever fearless, leaped to his feet, beaming and eager. The instructor clipped the static line to Paul's rip cord and threw open the side door, filling our ears with the nasal whine of the engines. Paul sat on the floor by the open door, dangling his legs outside and spreading his arms to grip the sides of the opening. On the signal from the pilot, the instructor slapped Paul on the back, shouting "JUMP!" and Paul was gone. The umbilical cord connecting him to the plane pulled taut then slacked limp. The instructor leaned out to check Paul's progress. He gave thumbs up to the pilot and reeled in the line.

"WHO'S NEXT?" he asked, his voice straining over roaring engines and howling wind.

I was suddenly worried about Paul. I had visions of Mae West, emergency chutes, and crash landings. I needed to verify with my own eyes that he was floating safely to earth. I inched closer to the door hoping to find him in the distance, dangling happily beneath a white bubble. Then I heard the static line snap onto my chute.

"SIT DOWN." The instructor pointed to the floor by the open door. "LEGS OUT."

I did as told. My legs were immediately swept backwards by the wind, pant legs flapping violently. My mouth was as dry as toast. There was nothing between me and the ground but 4,000 feet of air and a parachute that I was sure had been packed by a twenty-year-old with a severe hangover.

It suddenly dawned on me that this whole adventure was a bad idea. I was prepared to suffer feeling the sissy in this squadron of adrenaline junkies—anything would be better than releasing my white-knuckled grip on the plane. I was about to excuse myself from their suicidal ritual when the instructor, who must have sensed my hesitation, shouted "JUMP!" and slapped my back with sufficient gusto to dislodge me from my perch.

Perhaps you've had a nightmare in which you are falling interminably into an abyss—then you awaken with a start, clutching your mattress. The first seconds of falling from the plane were just like that. Only rather than awakening, frightened, in the warmth of my bed, there was a sharp yank as the static line reached its limit.

Suddenly, there were yards and yards of parachute pouring past my head. The risers smacked noisily against my helmet as they extended from the pack behind me, pushing the ill-fitting helmet over my eyes. My only desire, my only thought at that precise moment, was to see my parachute wide open above me. Chute, beloved chute, blessed roundness, life-giving dome! But I couldn't see a bloody thing. When I realized that the helmet had slid forward, I reached up to rock it back, again looking skyward. But the risers whacked my helmet back over my eyes.

At this point, something inside me snapped. My mind blanked and my body drooped. A soothing numbness enveloped me. Shock is like that.

When the chute had expanded and the risers stopped flapping, I pushed the helmet back one more time and was at last able to see the graceful white circle floating above me. To my considerable delight, I was not dropping like a stone with only a flimsy motorcycle helmet to cushion the impact. But I couldn't help but look up a few more times just to be sure.

I was so anxiously verifying and re-verifying the state of my chute that I neglected to notice my drift. A disembodied voice brought me back to the present.

"Jumper number 2—Left toggle!"

I had forgotten about the walkie-talkie strapped onto my emergency chute. Again it crackled.

"Jumper number 2—LEFT TOGGLE!"

I looked down, but couldn't find the field by the runway. I pulled hard on the left toggle and the world below me began to rotate counter-clockwise. As I looked at the ground far below, I had the distinct impression that I was not descending at all. Given the altitude and the slow rate of descent, your movement from moment to moment makes hardly a dent in your overall distance from the earth, giving the impression of hanging motionless in the air.

I felt suspended in time. The only sound was the breeze whistling softly through my helmet. Below me a patchwork quilt of autumn colors extended in every direction, with shimmering golden sugar maples and dark green pines, everywhere punctuated with blazing orange and deep ruby red. There were open fields and checkerboard plots of farmland. I could see the eight lanes of the New York Thruway to the South, heading west toward Syracuse.

I was interrupted again by the walkie-talkie.

"Jumper number 2—LET GO of the left toggle!"

I was way off course. In fact, I had no idea where I was supposed to land.

But landing was becoming an issue. As I continued my descent, previously fuzzy details were coming into focus. Below me was not an expansive green field, but a clot of trees. The last thing you want to do is to straddle a branch on your way down. I wrapped my ankles around each other the way they'd told us and pictured myself rattling through the thinner branches, snap-snap-crack, until I lodged in the tree, suspended by my crotch, waiting hours for a rescue team to find me. This was not what I signed up for.

But I had misjudged my forward velocity. I overshot the trees and was heading for a flat brown patch of tended field. As I closed in I could see lighter and darker stripes, as if something had recently been planted or harvested. It looked pretty safe, assuming the farmer wasn't in the habit of shooting trespassers.

The field was growing rapidly. I couldn't take my eyes off the ground as it rushed towards my dangling feet. But something seemed wrong: I was moving much faster than our practice jumps from five feet had prepared me for. I braced myself for the impact, but as warned, I miscalculated and smashed into the cold, hard earth with the grace of a horsefly smacking a windowpane. Despite the tall boots, my right ankle twisted below me as I crumpled into a heap. My chute followed a moment later, shrouding me in fabric and tangles of rope.

I sat, motionless, for several minutes, in shock but thankful to be back on *terra firma.* Then I realized that something smelled like shit. Not dogpile quantities—large farm animal quantities. I swam against the fabric until I found daylight. My only stroke of luck of the day: I had landed on one of the strips of packed dirt between ankle-deep rows of manure.

I stood to gather my chute, but collapsed immediately, clutching my aching ankle and swearing like a truck driver. I cursed my injury, my helmet, my ex-friend Paul, and my own stupidity for engaging in this masochistic boondoggle. The office, and with it my ride home, was nowhere in sight. I was sitting in the middle of some farmer's bean field with a rapidly swelling ankle and an acre of parachute for which I was personally responsible.

Above me, I could see one of the experts floating gracefully earthward in his parasail, a wing-like device that is far more navigable than a simple round parachute. I watched him disappear beyond a clump of pines, surely just yards from the office. But a good half mile from where I sat.

I briefly considered my options. I refused to compound the disgrace of my lame-ass jump by calling the instructor on the walkie-talkie to come fetch me. From my seated position, I tugged at the lines, gathering my chute toward me. But the field tugged back, its twigs and branches mocking my misfortune. I stood on my good leg, heaving the risers and tearing the chute free from its snag, half-hoping I ripped a hole in it. I had no idea the thing was so huge! I finally pulled together a pile of fabric about the size and manageability of three weeks' worth of laundry and began limping in the direction of the airport.

Through some painful experimentation, I discovered that if I kept my right foot pointed like a ballerina and hopped with my left leg, I could manage a stumbling shuffle vaguely reminiscent of walking. After forty-five minutes of wincing and cussing, I reached the office.

I struggled to hold back the tears as I opened the door to find my co-jumpers in a celebratory mood. I needed soothing. Instead, I got Paul.

"Wasn't that awesome?" Paul, of course, had steered his chute like a champ, right into the center of the field by the runway, landed with textbook form, and had been waiting for me for close to an hour. I dumped my parachute at his feet, like delivering the corpse of a vanquished foe. In his exuberance, he apparently failed to notice my limp or my scowl.

"Wanna go again?"

RICHARD PLEVIN writes prose and software wherever he and his peripatetic family find themselves.

DEBRA TASH

Completing the Circuit

Emile Nolde.
The Mulatto.
Oil on canvas, 1913.
The Busch-Reisinger Museum, Harvard University Art Museums.
G. David Thompson Fund.

LOURDES, FRANCE: A HONKY-TONK PLACE, part swap meet, part holy Mecca, a place unashamed of its split personality. As a well-traveled cynic I was talked into a tour of France by my in-laws, a fast paced, see everything—but really don't experience anything—type of arrangement. So this is how I came to Lourdes in September, near the end of the pilgrim season.

Before the rains started and the tourists dried up, I walked along streets packed with browsers perusing knickknacks of questionable taste in countless shops: the most outrageous souvenir being the plastic water bottles with the head of the Holy Mother. Her crowned pate, acting as the cap, twists off so the faithful can fill their jugs full of the famous Lourdes water—the most prized keepsake. There were all sorts about me: Italian, French, flocks of Americans who had come just for the experience of seeing the holy spot that had once been a quiet village.

The area beyond Lourdes is spectacular. There are the sturdy Pyrenees mountains coated with greenery, dips of carpeted valleys, stretches of farmland, and the silent rock walls of a medieval fortress overlooking the twisted streets of the flamboyant village below. What a backwater it must have been in Bernadette Soubirous' time, poor and isolated. Now it's a regular tourist stop, a hub for the faithful and the sightseer alike. For me it was just another place to visit. I hadn't a spiritual inkling of what to expect.

The entrance to the Massabielle grotto, where the fourteen-year-old, impoverished Bernadette first saw the Virgin, is to the side of the present day sanctuary erected on the site. That sanctuary is a flashy basilica, gilded and a bit overwrought, with a towering spire on top. Walking around the church, I came to the grotto. There I waited for the opportunity to amble about the shallow rock cavity. Pillar candles burned on either side, large luminescent beacons to my left, the offerings of pilgrim groups, to my right tall thin tappers representing individual hopes. When I drew near the grotto I noticed the rock had been worn smooth. Millions of hands had touched it, fingers slipping along its surface. Beneath a glass window buried in the grotto floor a small stream of running water could be seen. This was the place where the Virgin instructed Bernadette to dig in the dry soil. The girl who had been told by her mother to gather wood for her family's poor hearth experienced a profound revelation there.

Outside is a row of taps, more than I could count. Here the hopeful take those plastic, Holy Mother bedecked jugs and fill them with the healing water of Lourdes. They wash their limbs in it, splash it upon their faces, mouths moving in silent prayer. Is this really the power of Lourdes, its attraction? I went away that afternoon perplexed.

That night I was asked by my in-laws to accompany them to the candlelight procession. There is a balcony along the front of the basilica. The roadway on either side arches across the brow of the church to form that asphalt veranda. We stood on it, looking out on the thousands upon thousands below, all holding long tapered candles. Each candle had a paper shield to keep the wind from extinguishing its dancing flame. A few of those shields caught fire, flaring with brilliance until the unruly light was stamped out. On loudspeakers a Mass was being broadcast to those outside the church. Each prayer would be said and repeated again and again in different languages. Then the crowd below would sing, raising their candles when the words, *Ave Maria,* were uttered.

Soon the procession began with hundreds of people being pushed on stretchers, then those in wheelchairs, and finally the rest, walking behind, all holding candles. Thousands of candles became a molten river, light moving until all those people formed that long river that was turning back to its place of origin. It glowed, rippling brilliance. Beyond the river were the closed souvenir shops, the empty streets where so many had jostled along during the day. The medieval castle, lit with streamers of light from electric bulbs, looked down from its perch on the hillside above. Here prisoners were housed in the seventeenth and eighteenth centuries.

I looked at the scene before me. It struck the cynic in me hard. Weren't we prisoners as well? Or were we free? The river of light, waxen amber, completed itself as I watched, a long oblong circle, no ends, no beginnings. Here we gathered: the hopeful, the sightseer, the true believer and, of course, the doubter. The truth came on me, flooding my heart. Somewhere, in us all is that river, pure light given from God, returned, a complete circuit of love. It moved me, touched the core of my soul, all that light and all those who hoped in that dark, glittering night. We were no different from one another, the sightseer and the pilgrim. We'd come to this place, a place where a young girl knelt in the dirt, dug with her bare hands and found water where none flowed before. All that I had seen during the day, all I witnessed through the night had started with individual faith. And the answer to faith's prayer isn't in one place or another. It occurred to me then it's really in the yearning heart, one very much like that rich heart of a young girl who had really believed. I smiled. Even a cynic can learn the lesson Lourdes has to offer: to really be healed we need to fill our hearts with the Living Water delivered to us upon a river of purest light.

DEBRA TASH is vice-president of a small manufacturing firm and a member of the Archaeological Institute of America, University of California, Santa Barbara Chapter. She arranges and leads field trips for local home-school groups to instill in them a love of history, and volunteers at the J. Paul Getty Center as a storyteller. Currently she conducts tours at the Ventura County Maritime Museum.

SUZANNE GOLD

Encountering Sainte Suzanne

Suzanne Gold. *Sainte Suzanne.* Church of Sainte Suzanne, Normandy, France. Photograph, 1988.

DURING A MONTH-LONG HOME EXCHANGE in Brittany, my husband, Dan, and I visited Combourg Castle, a feudal fortress. Dark and spooky, it was once the home of François-René Chateaubriand, one of France's most beloved, if gloomy, writers. Our guide read from the young Chateaubriand's account of meeting the ghost of a pirate, watching it fade until only its peg-leg remained. She showed the shriveled mummy of a cat found during restoration of a tower wall where it had been buried alive a thousand years before to ward off evil spirits.

Afterward, the castle's moody ambience haunted my dreams. The Frenchman's depression had triggered my own. Chateaubriand and I had both been raised in bleak homes. His fear of the guillotine reflected my family's ancestral dread of the Nazis, the pogroms, and myriad oppressions throughout history. All my life, I'd struggled to free myself from the effects of my extremely dysfunctional family—debilitating fear, lack of confidence, and a discouraging sense that it was up to me to make everything right. By this time, I knew I'd made progress but still felt hopeless about ever escaping the influence.

The stirred-up emotions played themselves out as I slept. *Frustration, dread... Inching my sister's car through a crowd who stubbornly refused to move out of the way. In the shotgun seat, stubborn and oblivious, she flirted recklessly.*

After a particularly bad night of almost no sleep, *I dreamed of a ghost playing a typically haunting classical piece on my piano. Then a flashlight clattered down from the chimney into the fireplace, followed by a pair of reaching, grasping mechanical hands. I awoke screaming.*

We'd planned a visit to Monet's house in Normandy, and I was hoping a change of scene would break the eerie spell. As I mapped the route, I noticed a town called Sainte Suzanne along the way. We passed a highway sign announcing Sainte Suzanne, calling it a "Cité Mediéval." Being a Suzanne myself, though from a Jewish family in Philadelphia, I was intrigued. I told Dan I hoped to stop there on our return trip.

Monet's cheerful home and studio, curved bridges, the riot of color and fragrance in his manicured gardens, were enchanting. In the evening, we drank homemade cider and fed baguette crumbs to black swans in the courtyard pond at our farmhouse lodgings. Later, I had a richly woven dream: *I was flying home from France, then suddenly, as if by teleportation, being in a Manhattan apartment without luggage, purse or credit cards, and panicking about how to get back to California. An interior voice told me not to worry, that I was whisked off the plane to shield me from something dangerous about to happen.*

Although I didn't realize it at the time, that was my first encounter with the saint herself.

On the return drive to Brittany, Dan and I aimed for a picnic lunch in Sainte Suzanne. On joining the autoroute, we stopped at a rest area. While I used les toilettes, Dan browsed the boutique. This is a guy who can't tolerate more than five minutes in any store that doesn't sell hardware. But the language difference turned it into an adventure in culture. We'd whiled away almost an hour before he decided to buy himself a khaki fisherman's vest with a dozen pockets.

Within minutes of merging onto the highway, we were stopped dead in a traffic jam. The official autoroute radio station reported that only moments before, a tiny Renault had swerved out of control and hit a tanker truck. Both overturned and exploded. It was a hot

Friday afternoon preceding the summer's biggest holiday weekend, and the road to Brittany's beaches was now closed in both directions.

Sweltering and powerless, we read books, picnicked in the car instead of at Sainte Suzanne, and tried to maintain a sense of humor. Hours later, traffic began to crawl off the toll road at the nearest exit. Gendarmes, the French police, directed traffic through small villages and over narrow country roads to the next on-ramp. Every few miles, local samaritans offered free liter bottles of cold mineral water.

It was after six when we reached Sainte Suzanne, glowing in the golden light as though it was God's favorite place. Ancient buildings encircled a hilltop with a river at its feet. The cobbled streets were deserted, but the small tourist office was still open, as if they'd been waiting for us. The friendly women inside were delighted to learn that I shared the name of their town's patron saint. They showered me with photos and pamphlets. The museum was probably closed by then, they said, but the walk along the ramparts to the church was beautiful.

Like most French villages in summer, Sainte Suzanne was ablaze with flowers. Two chateaus lorded over timeworn stone houses. Religious icons peeked out of recesses in their walls. The surrounding countryside was studded with ancient standing stones, small farms, and forests.

The museum's studded plank door gaped open. Dan and I poked our heads inside. It was shadowy and cool with thick dark beams propping up a low stone ceiling. There was no one in sight.

As we debated if we should go in, a raspy female voice with a Brooklyn accent welcomed us. It was the curator, an expatriate American. She offered a quick outline of the town's history. I asked about Suzanne's saintly qualities. The director said something vague about her being the patron of engaged couples and was flipping through a book to check. I was waiting, taking in the atmosphere, when I felt something brush my hair, my shoulder, then heard the gentle plop of it hitting the floor.

At my feet, in this medieval room with not a flower in sight, was a morning glory. I lifted the fragile blossom and tucked it behind my ear. My body quivered as if an electric current was rushing through it. It occurred to me that Sainte Suzanne was trying to get my attention, but I dismissed it as a ridiculous idea.

Soon the curator shooed us out, pointing us in the direction of the church in the square at the top of the hill. The exterior of Sainte Suzanne's sanctuary was weathered and grey, but within, pristine white stone soared in the dim candlelight. In the alcove with a statue of Suzanne, a prayer "for those without one of their own," was posted above the votives. Loosely translated, it was:

Even though I don't know what to say,
and I don't know how to pray,
and I have so little time to spend in prayer,
I light this candle to leave part of myself with God,
who knows my joys and sorrows
and holds me in tenderness."

I dropped a few francs in the box, lit a candle and whispered the prayer, in the French. The tingling resumed. Behind the altar, three stained-glass story windows gleamed. Stepping closer to Sainte Suzanne's, I translated each caption, reflecting on her adventures. One scene in particular took my breath away. In it, Suzanne kneels at the feet of an angel, whose arm stretches out to ward off a Roman soldier. Framed by petal shapes reminiscent of a morning glory's, her image radiates faith.

I could use some of that, I thought. I focused my telephoto on just that section, praying for enough light to capture it, and snapped the picture. I was wandering around drinking it all in when Dan collected me for the ride home. No Combourg castle ghosts haunted me that night. Over coffee and croissants at the village cafe the next morning, we struggled to decipher a newspaper account about the collision on the autoroute, which had been much more tragic and dangerous than we knew. The car's occupants had died instantly as their vehicle burst into flames. The trucker was killed while he struggled in vain to prevent the fire from igniting his cargo of gasoline. Until the ensuing inferno had cooled sufficiently, fire crews could work only on keeping it away from a nearby natural gas storage facility.

I felt fortunate that we'd been far enough behind for safety. My next thought was that luck had nothing to do with it— that Sainte Suzanne's spirit had safeguarded us even before we'd consciously made her acquaintance. That the mere intention of contacting her initiated a relationship, and my dream of being whisked off the endangered airplane was a metaphoric message, a preview of how she would keep us dawdling at the roadside boutique to protect us from the catastrophe. Another delicious vibration snaked through me, as if the metaphorical Uroboros serpent was climbing my spine, partnering with Sainte Suzanne to energize each chakra and set the very molecules of my body dancing.

On the next market day in Rennes, the nearest big city, we had the film from our Normandy excursion developed. Every photo I'd shot in the church was too dim to make out, except Sainte Suzanne and the angel. It was perfectly balanced, brilliant and crystalline. I propped it against my bedside lamp, asking for her help with the castle's disturbing apparitions. The next dream I could remember was long and complicated. First, meeting a childhood friend at a conference, telling her about France and St. Suzanne. Then driving in San Francisco, up a potholed, gravelly street so steep pedestrians had to crawl and claw their way up. I turned a corner and found myself in a doctor's office trying to help a man find insulin for his dying daughter. Then a bomb threat, ambulances, an explosion . . . searching frantically for the medicine while things fall apart. Sainte Suzanne was turning me away from the struggle, guiding me to healing in the midst of chaos.

Before leaving France, we spent a few days in Paris, where I dreamt of finding money, jewelry, and chocolates, then driving a car precariously balanced atop a narrow wall. Next thing I knew, I was breastfeeding a baby I'd just borne, who was growing so fast I could see it. I felt that I'd been given a miracle. When I awoke, I considered trusting my intuition of a connection with Sainte Suzanne.

Back in the US, I searched for an "official" version of Sainte Suzanne's story. I corresponded with Kathy Rubenstein, who was cataloging saints for St. Patrick's Church in Washington, D.C. In my local library, I found Sainte Suzanne's entry in John Delaney's *Dictionary of Saints.* It said the Roman Emperor Diocletian wanted Suzanne to marry Maximianus Herculeus, his son-in-law and co-ruler. Her uncles, both Diocletian's courtiers, were dispatched to bring Suzanne to Rome for the marriage, but she refused to forsake her devotion to her vision of the sacred. Her faith was so compelling that her uncles abandoned their mission and converted to Christianity. Enraged, Diocletian ordered Suzanne and her entire family killed.

I wasn't crazy about the ending, but the part about sticking to your guns for what you feel is true inspired me. I was sitting on a stool in the aisle that housed the religion books, contemplating the parallels in my own life, and recalled that early in my relationship with Dan, a friend had told me of an Old Testament story called "Daniel and the Trial of Susanna." Close by were several Bibles, so I decided to look that one up, too.

The story was actually from the Apochrypha, considered a more mythical document than the Bible. Susanna was a fabled beauty whose rich, wise husband was so esteemed by the Jews of Babylon that his spacious residence doubled as the courthouse. During court business, Susanna retreated to her garden.

Two of the judges, obsessed with Susanna's charm, were wont to spy on her. One day, they launched a blackmail plan. They said unless she had sex with them, they'd testify to seeing her in the garden fornicating shamelessly with a handsome young man, an offense punishable with death by stoning.

Susanna told them she preferred to trust God with her fate rather than appeasing their hypocrisy. She was brought to trial and found guilty, but the prophet Daniel unexpectedly intervened. Although relatively unknown in the community at the time and unacquainted with Susanna, he was moved by spirit to come to her defense. His argument for further investigation so impressed the officials that they authorized it. Daniel questioned each accuser separately and exposed contradictions in their testimony that destroyed their credibility. Susanna was freed, the charlatans themselves were executed for bearing false witness, and Daniel became the wise and holy man in the lion's den.

Susanna, Suzanne. Same name, same theme. I envisioned an ongoing archetype based on a series of women throughout time who risked their lives, and sometimes lost them, for what they believed, and who, for me, are symbolized in Sainte Suzanne. Though physical, she experienced Spirit directly. My encounter with her enabled me to sense her beside me, inside me, lending support, nurturance and purity of spirit. Like a beacon lighting the way to peace, her presence enlivens my faith in my own personal, conscious connection with the Eternal.

SUZANNE GOLD, who holds a master's degree in clinical psychology from Temple University, is the author of *Daddy's Girls*, an autobiographical novel of love, spirit and redemption, which was awarded the Gold Medal by *Foreword* magazine's 2001 Book-of-the-Year Awards in the General Fiction Category. Her book *Being Yourself: Twenty-Four Ways to See the Light, is* a self-help book that promotes spiritual awareness and peace of mind. Her writing has appeared in the *San Francisco Chronicle, SF Weekly, Northern Journeys,* and online at *LifetimeTV.com, Writers' Web Designs, Arcamax Newsletter for Women,* and *Artrageous Women.*

JANE EKLUND

A Small Blessing

So what if you can't name what comes next.
You have the green heron, balanced on one stick
of a leg, knee-deep in the lake. You have
the mud-puddle song of the bullfrog,
the ache of new moon in the afternoon blue,
the bee burrowing in the magnolia's womb.
Listen: Sitting cross-legged on a warm porch
in mid spring is enough, it's enough
of a life's work. So what, so what
if you cannot name it.

JANE EKLUND's poems have appeared or are forthcoming in *Poetry Northwest*, *Calyx*, and *The Sun*. She works as editor of a weekly newspaper in Peterborough, New Hampshire.

Piet Mondrian, *Composition No. 7 (Façade).* Oil on canvas, 47½×39⅞ in., 1914. Kimbell Art Museum, Fort Worth, Texas.

Unpacking the Latin

The New Translation of Swedenborg's *Divine Providence*

THE THEOLOGICAL VOLUMES of Emanuel Swedenborg (1688–1772) have been treasured by countless Western writers, thinkers, and artists over the last two-hundred and fifty years. Swedenborg's thought has had particular impact in America, where his nonsectarian teachings about freedom of belief and action, universal brotherhood, the importance of a useful life, and the continuing betterment of the human spirit have resonated with prevailing ideas of democracy.

Swedenborg's detailed descriptions of spiritual realms are unique in history and more timely than ever in today's age of spiritual exploration. His remarkable experiences of a heavenly kingdom intended for everyone by a God of infinite love, mercy, and wisdom offer a positive framework for understanding life's meaning. One of his most popular titles has been *Angelic Wisdom Concerning Divine Providence,* which (since Swedenborg wrote in Latin) was originally published as *Sapienta Angelica de Divina Providentiae,* in 1764. The first English translation appeared in 1790 in Manchester, where there were many British readers of Swedenborg. The 1790 translation was the work of an Anglican rector, John Clowes, who preached Swedenborgian concepts to his Church of England parishioners. Mr. Clowes, in fact, translated many of Swedenborg's works into English.

George Dole, who has just completed the task of newly translating Swedenborg's *Divine Providence,* graduated from Yale University with a bachelor's degree in classics and from Oxford with a master's degree in Hebrew. He holds a doctorate in Assyriology from Harvard University. He has also translated Swedenborg's *Heaven and Hell* and

Divine Love and Wisdom. George says about the New Century Edition,

> Over the last two centuries, divine providence has been translated afresh several times. Next spring my new translation will appear, the first since 1963. It is part of Swedenborg's entire theological oeuvre of some twenty-five volumes, which Swedenborg Foundation Publishers is now just commencing to produce in a new edition—a formidable task! We intend that the "New Century" edition will convey the richness and variety of Swedenborg's prose, presenting his works in a modern English that retains the dignity and simplicity of the original Latin. Each of the volumes will be introduced and annotated by scholars expert in Swedenborgian studies and Western intellectual history.
>
> I will not take you along the path that brought me to the enterprise, but I believe that there are some currents of thought that favor the project and that there is a serendipitous confluence over which we have no control.
>
> There are the advances in the study and understanding of language. Descriptive linguistics is to the translator what a tool kit is to the mechanic, enabling us to take sentences apart and see how they work. Semantics explores the mysterious interface between words and meanings. The more closely the language of Swedenborg's theological corpus is examined, the more overwhelming is the impression of its simplicity. The larger that conclusion looms, the more intense is the resolve to translate that simplicity into English, and to do so without loss of the extraordinary intelligence of the texts. It is not a case of "dumbing things down," not at all. It is purely a matter of fidelity.
>
> Technology has eased our task immensely. Our sophisticated search program saves us countless hours of page-turning. We can look up words in the British lexicon of Swedenborg's Latin on screen, as well. We have facsimiles of the first editions on CD—and all of this, the search program, the lexicon, and the first editions, can be carried around in a laptop computer. When the New Century Edition editorial committee leaves our meetings, and we go our several ways, email takes over, and we continue to support and to learn from each other.
>
> Then there is vibrant interface between theology and psychology. Swedenborg wrote about the human soul—its strengths and weaknesses, its tragedies and triumphs. In our own time, we share in a cultural awakening to the everyday mysteries of our human nature; so quite naturally, as we try to understand what is said about the process of being human, we look within ourselves.
>
> There has been a growing restiveness within the established Swedenborgian community with the language of translations dating from a century past. Further, there has been a growing

awareness that although Swedenborg may well be regarded as unique, he is not alone. He did not invent the inner landscape that we find in his works. Others have seen or sensed many of the spiritual realities that he describes with such care, and have expressed them in the languages of their own cultures. The task of the translator is not to introduce the reader to some new and alien world but to bring the familiar into a new and clearer light. We do not have to make the world conform to Swedenborgian theology, simply to see the profound and beautiful ways in which it does.

SWEDENBORG'S 1764 WORK ON DIVINE PROVIDENCE is a unique statement of the way God works in the world. It confronts the questions posed by the authors you have just read in this Chrysalis anthology. They pose the same questions that have dogged humankind since ancient times: How can we truly be free in a world in which a Supreme Being actively participates? Why is there evil in such a world? How is our experience in the physical world balanced by our experience in the spiritual realm after the death of the body? How should we best adapt ourselves to live in peace, rather than in conflict, with God and with one another? Although Swedenborg addresses these issues in the context of intellectual history and of the thinking of his own times, his answers are unlike those of other thinkers and mystics. Writing as he did at the commencement of the early modern period—which is in fact our own period in history—his answers remain cogent for us today.

God, says Swedenborg, created the world from divine love, using divine wisdom. The meaning of that fact, which we often find all too easy to trivialize, is that we, sharing in that creation, are beings of love and wisdom as well. The evil we do and suffer is a result of our remove from the divine, for God has given us the freedom to choose to live in harmony with divine love and wisdom or in disunity with it. This freedom is one of the ways divine providence works to bring us back into harmony with God; another way is through our rationality. No matter how far from God we stand, no matter how sundered from our own happiness we are, no matter how evil, freedom and rationality remain in us, constantly at work. As we form the core values of our lives—what Swedenborg calls our chief "loves"—divine providence, working through our freedom and rationality, leads us on to the fulfillment of divine purpose.

Even evil serves its role in this providence, by teaching us the value of what is good. Not only that, it provides one end of the continuum of our choices, making our freedom a fact instead of an illusion. Our lives are thus real, not a game we play in a determined universe in which the unhealthy consequences of our choices can all be reversed in a moment of shallow deathbed repentance. God allows evil out of love for us—a paradox we cannot understand unless we take responsibility for who we are, how we act, and what we want to become.

Swedenborg sees our existence as stretching infinitely far forward. Our lives are formative, but after transition from life we continue in the roles we have chosen. Those who have gained some unity with God remain close to the divine; those who have been at more of a remove find their eternal roles at a similar remove after death; and those who have found their delight in evil dwell in hell, by their own choice. Curiously enough, the closer we are to God, the more free we become, because the freedom to choose good is a wise freedom, while the freedom to choose evil is one that is unwise. Freedom, rationality, love, and wisdom are thus linked in divine providence.

The populating of the spiritual world is the key function of creation. God, as an infinite being, interacts with our finiteness through the vast image of him we collectively form, which Swedenborg terms "the universal human." This collective being does not have a specific "shape," as it does not exist in space and time (life after death is beyond these dimensions), but it corresponds to the Divine image.

Having sketched the overall theory and purpose behind providence, Swedenborg explains the laws by which it operates: According to the first of these, if we act in freedom and in accordance with reason, we enter a state of tentative reformation and ultimately full-blown regeneration, recentering our lives around our love for God and others. Even though God is constantly flowing into us, keeping us alive, we must act as if we were independent of God, and in so acting give meaning to the freedom God has given to us.

Another law holds that if we actively work to remove the failings of our outer self, the healing of the inner self will follow. With great psychological acuteness, Swedenborg points out how the pleasure of our failings reinforces itself. If we do not find in our rationality the reason to desist from taking that one drink too many, for example, we will discover that the pleasure of that drink only reinforces our dependence. Reformation and regeneration require active work, active avoidance of the ills we are trying to mend.

Yet another law holds that we cannot be compelled to believe in and love God by forces outside ourselves. It is in ourselves that we must find our belief and love. Other laws emphasize the role of the Word of God in moving us toward regeneration and stress the importance of our acting in an awareness of divine providence, though its overall operation remains largely concealed.

Swedenborg then turns to a consideration of the value of our foresight or prudence. Most importantly, he says, we should know that divine providence extends into the least details of our world. It works even in the unknown depths of our subconscious mind—fortunately, because if it did not, we would be unable to function even minimally. Thus human prudence, for all we tend to value it, is not a useful guide. To use a metaphor, when we employ our prudence, we are like the paddler at the bow of the canoe who thinks the boat moves under his or her direction, while in fact it is the paddler at the stern who guides it through the rapids. All the same, by acting as if our prudence is valuable, we can use it to second the workings of divine providence in our lives.

Divine providence, continues Swedenborg, is focused on eternal matters. The minor, temporal matters of our life in this world are not significant except insofar as they align themselves with the purpose of the Eternal. This is the key to our course of action in this world, and to how we should view both the obstacles and advancements we encounter in daily life.

Divine providence allows us an understanding of the truth that comes out of faith and of that good that arises from caring about God and others. This understanding is precisely in accordance with our ability to hold it in heart and mind to the end of our lives. If we see more of Divine truth and good than we can appreciate, in our contempt for it we only harm ourselves. Divine providence is thus self-regulating as it reveals itself within us.

In the concluding chapters of the book, Swedenborg deals with the problem of evil and the question of whether or not we are predestined to some particular course. Evil, he says, is essentially the pleasure we feel when we act and think in violation of the divine pattern; good is the pleasure we feel when we are in harmony with that divine pattern. We each have the freedom to be re-formed and regenerated so that we move into greater harmony with the Divine. The laws of the world, in Swedenborg's explanation, are not so mysterious. They do not function in a manner contrary to divine providence. Not even God does so, because to violate the laws of the universe God has established would be to act against the Divine itself.

In *Divine Providence,* Swedenborg outlines the vast wholeness of the workings of the Divine, the way divine love and wisdom operate in the cosmos. In that wholeness we see the mysteriously sharp fragments and the baffling loose ends of our existence now subsumed and gathered together; and from them arises, in splendor, both meaning and beauty, where before there was only meaninglessness and ugliness. After following the wendings of Swedenborg's direct, heartfelt, and simple prose we suddenly feel we have got the gist of the universe for the first time. We see ourselves moving forward, on a path uniquely our own, fully able to choose what we will be. Rather than being doomed to live as perennial outsiders in God's cosmos, we discover we are free to find our own place in its pattern.

GEORGE F. DOLE is a Swedenborgian minister who lives in Bath, Maine. "It seems to me," George says, "that one area in which this country is in the lead, is in dealing with religious pluralism: Swedenborg's respect for all lives lived according to faith in the divine emphasizes the Swedenborgian tenet that, despite cultural differences, there is great unity underlying the world's religions. In the 'Welcome' card for our church I wrote that we are Christian and Bible-centered and that we believe that there is a path to heaven in every religion, so if we can help a Methodist be a better Methodist or a Muslim be a better Muslim, we've done our job." STUART SHOTWELL (who summarized Swedenborg's *Divine Providence* in this essay) is the managing editor of the entire new edition of Swedenborg's published theological works, a publishing effort projected to take more than a dozen years. Dr. Shotwell's summary is based on GREGORY JOHNSON's introduction to the new Dole translation. Dr. Johnson is on the faculty of the Swedenborgian House of Studies at the Pacific School of Religion in Berkeley, California.